"I heartily recommend this  -use
book. Pediatrician Michelle E riety
of methods for accessing the power of mindfulness to manage
stress and cultivate happiness and well-being. Any parent of a
stressed-out child should find something useful and sustaining
here."

> —Jeffrey Brantley, MD, DFAPA, author of *Calming*
> *Your Anxious Mind* and founder and director of the
> mindfulness-based stress reduction (MBSR) program
> at Duke Integrative Medicine in Durham, NC

"Easy-to-read, practical tips tested through personal experience and illustrated with inspiring stories. I will recommend
this book to families interested in learning how to use mindful
practices to help kids master stress."

> —Kathi Kemper, MD, MPH, FAAP, author of *Mental*
> *Health Naturally* and *The Holistic Pediatrician*

"This book is written in friendly, accessible language. It offers
parents and children proven skills for dealing with stress and
creating good mental health."

> —Amy Saltzman, MD, director of Still Quiet Place
> and the Association for Mindfulness in Education

"Michelle Bailey has created a highly applicable and practical
hands-on book for parents raising children in the twenty-first
century. Not only will the skills in this book be helpful to children, but they will also benefit the parents themselves. It is
with great pleasure that I recommend this book."

> —Gina M. Biegel, MA, LMFT, psychotherapist and
> author of *The Stress Reduction Workbook for Teens*

Parenting Your Stressed Child

10 Mindfulness-Based Stress Reduction
Practices to Help Your Child Manage Stress
and Build Essential Life Skills

MICHELLE L. BAILEY, MD, FAAP

NEW HARBINGER PUBLICATIONS, INC.

Distributed in Canada by Raincoast Books

Copyright © 2011 by Michelle L. Bailey
New Harbinger Publications, Inc.
5674 Shattuck Avenue
Oakland, CA 94609
www.newharbinger.com

Cover design by Amy Shoup
Acquired by Tesilya Hanauer
Edited by Karen O'Donnell Stein

Mixed Sources
Product group from well-managed
forests and other controlled sources
www.fsc.org Cert no. SW-COC-002283
FSC © 1996 Forest Stewardship Council

Printed in the United States of America

Library of Congress Cataloging-in-Publication Data

Bailey, Michelle L.
  Parenting your stressed child : 10 mindfulness-based stress reduction practices to help your child manage stress and build essential life skills / Michelle L. Bailey.
     p. cm.
  Includes bibliographical references.
  ISBN 978-1-57224-979-0 (pbk.) -- ISBN 978-1-57224-980-6 (pdf ebook)
  1. Stress in children. 2. Stress (Psychology) 3. Parenting--Handbooks, manuals, etc. I. Title.
  BF723.S75B35 2011
  649'.1--dc22

                        2011005862

13   12   11

10   9   8   7   6   5   4   3   2   1

First printing

Contents

■ Why I Wrote This Book ■ Got Stress? ■ Children Worry, Too ■ Adopting a Holistic Perspective ■ The World of Integrative Medicine ■ Physician, Heal Thyself ■ An Orientation: MBSR for Parents and Kids ■ What Is MBSR? ■ Kids Can Be Mindful, Too ■ The Value of Parents as Role Models ■ Ten Mindful Practices ■ How to Use This Book

Part III

■ The Importance of Practice ■ Building Healthy
Habits ■ Reinforcing New Concepts

■ Mindfulness for Kids ■ MBSR Programs, Books,
and Resources ■ Mindful Eating ■ Yoga for Kids
■ Programs for Health Care Professionals

Acknowledgments

Many people have graciously given of their time and talents to help inform the work contained in this book. I would first like to thank my patients and their parents who were open to exploring new approaches in medicine with me. I have learned as much from you as you have learned from me.

I want to express my thanks to Dr. Jon Kabat-Zinn, for his tireless efforts in educating the world about mindfulness-based stress reduction (MBSR). I consider it a privilege to help to spread the word about the benefits of MBSR and to help make it accessible to children and their families.

I wish to thank the team of MBSR instructors at Duke Integrative Medicine who brainstormed strategies to help adapt MBSR skills for children and supported my desire to bring this work forth: Mary Matthews Brantley, Dr. Maya McNeilly, Jeanne van Gemert, and Dr. Ron Vereen. A special thank-you goes to Duke Integrative Medicine's MBSR Director, Dr. Jeffrey Brantley. To you I owe a deep bow of gratitude for so freely sharing your wisdom with me and serving as such a wonderful role model, mentor, and friend—*Mahalo Nui Loa*.

I would also like to thank all those who played a part in helping me to establish a firm foundation in the field of integrative medicine: the leadership team of the Associate Fellowship Program in Integrative Medicine at the University of Arizona, Dr. Andrew Weil, Dr. Victoria Maizes, and Dr. Tieraona Low Dog; my treasured colleagues and friends in the Fellowship class of 2006; the visionaries at the Bravewell Collaborative, along with Dr. Sam Moon and Dr. Tracy Gaudet of Duke Integrative Medicine, for giving me the opportunity to train in integrative medicine; and my fearless and pioneering leaders in the department of pediatrics at Duke, Dr. Joseph St. Geme (chairman), Dr. Dennis Clements, and Dr. Elizabeth Landolfo. Thank you all for your generous support of my unique career path. To Dr. Larry Rosen, Dr. Sunita Vohra, and Dr. Tim Culbert, thank you for so generously sharing your wisdom and expertise with me; I appreciate each of you and value your friendship. And to Dr. Kathi Kemper, my mentor, colleague, and very dear friend, thank you for forging this path for pediatricians to provide truly holistic care to children and families.

. I am grateful for the openhearted collaboration of Marius Kluenger, Leslie Chapman, Jennifer Davis, Mike Belden, Kate Whetten, and Luililiaeli Mfangavo (affectionately known as Mama Lui) on our efforts to bring mindfulness to the children at Glenn Elementary school in Durham, N. C., and to the orphans and caregivers in Moshi, Tanzania.

Thanks so much to the wonderful editors and staff at New Harbinger—Wendy Millstine, for seeing the possibilities in a book such as this; Tesilya Hanauer, for your patience and guidance; and Jess Beebe and Karen Stein, for your thoughtful and gentle suggestions to refine and improve this work.

Finally, I would like to thank my family. Your love and support of my work has been nothing short of amazing. I am truly blessed to have such phenomenal people in my life. To my parents, George and Dorothy Bailey, thank you for loving me so generously: your love gave me the wings I needed to fly. I am fortunate to have a second set of parents, Bob and Elaine Shelton: your guidance and support over the years have meant more to me than you could ever imagine. To my son, Philip, you have been my greatest teacher in this lifetime thus far. You are an incredible gift to me and I am so very proud of the man and father that you have become. To my beloved Sharon, words cannot express how much I appreciate you: thank you for your endless encouragement and wonderful spirit and for choosing to share this journey with me.

Part I

Introduction

With the past, I have nothing to do;
nor with the future. I live now.

—Ralph Waldo Emerson

Parenting has been one of the greatest experiences of my life, and it has also been one of my greatest sources of stress. I never imagined I could love anyone as much as I love my son. I often wondered, "Am I doing a good enough job?" I wanted so much to give him the love, guidance, and sense of security that he needed in order to grow into a responsible and caring adult. My disappointments, frustrations, and difficulty in managing my own stress sometimes got in the way of my being the best parent I could be. At times I found myself stuck in the story that I'd created in my mind: the tale of a mother who just wasn't good enough. Mindfulness practice helped me to acknowledge where I was and how I was feeling in the moment. It reminded me that everything was okay. I knew that all was well and that these uncomfortable feelings would pass. Mindfulness gave me the choice to create a new story.

The intention of this book is to provide basic information and principles of mindfulness to promote a strong foundation for good mental health for yourself and your child. Rather than attempting to cover the entire topic of mindfulness, I aim to provide you with seeds to plant in your child's "garden of well-being." Tend to this garden by giving it your time and attention. Provide nourishment in the form of guidance, watering your child's mind with positive thoughts. Pull up any weeds that are sprouting; these are the negative thoughts that over time will choke out your child's joy and diminish her sense of self.

Children are vulnerable. They are dependent on their care-giving adults to provide a safe and loving place for them to grow and develop. So many children are experiencing incredible pain and suffering. They don't know how to articulate what they are feeling. They feel confused because they don't understand why they are behaving in a way that will result in negative consequences. They need help. They need instruction and guidance. Mindfulness can provide the skills that children require to build a stronger sense of self and resiliency, which will grow over their lifetime. It can also provide you, the parent, with the resources you need to more effectively support your child through these challenging times.

WHY I WROTE THIS BOOK

I wrote this book as one possible solution to the growing epidemic of stress-related illness and poor mental health in our kids today. This book is a first step toward supporting parents to teach children how to manage stress in a healthy way. As a parent, you will learn skills to help you identify the signs and symptoms of stress in your child. You will develop strategies to assist you in teaching your child how to better manage the stress in her life. And as you begin to incorporate these principles into your own life, you will be able to reinforce and model healthy coping strategies for your child.

I have experienced the power of developing a personal mindfulness practice firsthand. Learning to live in the present moment helped me to more effectively deal with my own stress in a healthy way. Teaching these skills to children and parents has had a positive impact in more ways than I ever could have imagined. Numerous parents have shared with me how much these practices have helped them personally. They report seeing differences in how their child handles stressful situations. It has also helped them approach their job as parent in a more effective way.

I firmly believe that these skills will also be of value to you And I'd love to hear your stories. I invite you to share your experiences with me about the value of the mindful practices in your life and the life of your child. You may contact me via e-mail at stories @parentingyourstressedchild.com or post on my website at www.parentingyourstressedchild.com.

Mindfulness offers a natural, healing-oriented solution that conventional medicine alone cannot. Mindfulness-based stress reduction (MBSR) has changed my life, and it gives me great joy to share the gift of mindfulness with you and your child. Here's to your health!

GOT STRESS?

When I was a young pediatrician, my primary objective was to assist parents in raising healthy, well-adjusted children. When children would come to the office with signs of illness, I wanted to make sure I knew what to do to help them recover as soon as possible. I wanted to have a positive impact on the families who trusted their kids' health to me. Armed with my prescription pad, stethoscope, and new medical knowledge, I felt confident that I had all the tools I needed to help solve the problems that parents presented. I had been taught how to treat an ear infection and how to manage constipation. What I wasn't as prepared for were the numerous concerns that parents raised related to increasing and overwhelming amounts of stress.

There seemed to be a growing sense of general "dis-ease" among the parents I saw. Many families were having financial difficulty resulting from job loss or the rising cost of basic necessities such as food and gas. Marital conflict led to rising tension within the home and sometimes to more permanent consequences such as divorce. Simply trying to get the kids fed, dressed, and off to school on time presented a daunting challenge to many young mothers and fathers, bringing with it a daily dose of stress.

More concerning to me was the fact that the children were also dealing silently with their own sources of stress. Stress can show up very differently in children than it does in adults. If you ask most children if they feel stressed, they are likely to respond with "no" or "I don't know." So how would you, as a parent, know if your child was stressed? Stress shows up in subtle ways in some kids: waking up frequently during the night when they used to sleep soundly, or earning Cs and Ds when they used to earn As and Bs, for example. Kids talked about the distraction and fatigue stemming from carrying their worries from class to class. In other cases, the stress was more obvious. Parents reported receiving calls at work from daycare providers or schoolteachers asking them to pick up their child due to disruptive behavior in the classroom. And no one could mistake the stress felt by a child who lashes out angrily at everyone and everything around her.

Chronic stress can cause significant disruption to a child's life. It may result in an inability to function. Evidence of chronic stress in kids often shows up as significant changes in your child's usual behavior. This includes increased sleepiness or insomnia, changes in eating patterns and/or appetite, and complaints of physical pain or discomfort (for example, frequent headaches). If you observe any of these common signs and symptoms of stress in your child, use this information to begin a conversation with her ("I've noticed that you seem to be having a hard time sleeping lately. Sometimes that happens to me when I have a lot on my mind. Why do you think you're not sleeping so well?"). Starting a dialogue in this nonthreatening way provides an opportunity for your child to safely explore feelings and emotions.

In some cases, a child may have a more severe response to traumatic events and situations. Intense stress reactions may include severe anxiety, depression, and thoughts of harming oneself or others. If you notice these extreme symptoms in your child, seek medical assistance immediately from your family doctor or mental health professional.

Children Worry, Too

As I saw more stressed children in my pediatric practice, I began to wonder what specific things children worried about and how they were handling their stress. I started asking kids two simple questions at each office visit. The first question was "What do you worry about?" Parents were surprised by the responses. Children as young as five or six years old described worrying about being teased on the school bus, not being liked by other kids at school or in the neighborhood, and Mommy and Daddy not having enough money. Older children were also stressed about family finances and the possibility of homelessness in addition to feeling insecure about their appearance as they headed into puberty. As children advanced to the next grade, they would express more concerns about academic pressures, including difficulty keeping up with schoolwork, earning low grades, and failing an important major exam. The second question was "What do you do to feel better when you're stressed or worried?" Kids often responded by listing several negative coping habits. The most common answers included going to sleep, eating even if they weren't hungry, watching TV, playing video games, or getting on the computer to zone out; in some cases they responded to stress with aggression by kicking or punching doors, walls, or even other people.

The advantage of asking children these two very simple questions is that it shed light on the dark feelings that kids often suffer with alone. Very rarely would I find a child who could not immediately come up with an answer to these questions. The concerns that children carry are very real. Many adults think of childhood as an idyllic time free from worry and stress, but obviously it's not. Children are people, and stress and worry are universal among all people. Increasing your awareness of what your child worries about allows you to provide guidance and support to her as she navigates this sometimes stormy route toward adulthood.

Ask yourself these same two questions as well. In the busyness of life, it is rather easy to distance yourself from thoughts and feelings that may result from increasing amounts of stress. Taking a moment to examine your stress management strategies, both healthy and unhealthy, is a big first step toward honestly facing how you're coping with what's on your plate.

As I began to reflect on the various stresses I was observing personally and professionally, I discovered there was a common thread that ran through my life as well as the lives of my patients and their parents. I saw that we were all worried about things that had happened in the past and things that might happen in the future. We were only rarely stopping to let our thoughts settle on what was happening now. We were not living in the present moment. Much of the stress that I observed manifested itself as feelings of disorganization, being overwhelmed, frustration, and at times despair. Unfortunately, our thoughts about the past or what would come in the future often exacerbated the negative emotions that came our way. It became apparent to me that children could benefit from learning stress management skills—including the ability to just live in the moment. Parents also expressed an interest in developing these skills for themselves.

ADOPTING A HOLISTIC PERSPECTIVE

As I pondered what I could do to better serve my patients and families, I also wondered what I could do to improve my own health. In 2005, I began a quest to learn how to improve my health naturally by changing my lifestyle habits. I came across the book *Eating Well for Optimum Health* by Dr. Andrew Weil (2000) and I found that I was inspired by the principles in this book that focused on food as medicine and on the natural healing ability of the body. While learning more about Dr. Weil, a graduate of Harvard Medical School, I discovered the field of integrative medicine.

The World of Integrative Medicine

Integrative medicine is a healing-oriented approach to health and well-being. It focuses on the individual rather than offering a "one size fits all" approach. Blending the best that conventional medicine and natural approaches have to offer, integrative medicine addresses the whole person, encompassing mind, body, and spirit. After learning about the Fellowship Program in Integrative Medicine at the University of Arizona, which Dr. Weil founded, I decided to apply; to my delight, I was not only accepted to the fellowship—a two-year distance learning program consisting of one thousand hours of curriculum in nutrition, botanical medicine, and mind-body medicine—but I also earned a competitive scholarship as a Bravewell Fellow. This allowed me to enroll in the fellowship program and train with integrative medicine physicians at Duke Integrative Medicine in Durham, North Carolina.

During my studies in the fellowship, I was introduced to MBSR. The basic eight-week class gave me a foundation of knowledge about the connection between the mind and the body, provided skills for learning how to live in the present moment, and emphasized the importance of cultivating non-judgmental awareness to promote feelings of well-being, stress reduction, and healthy stress management. However, my busy schedule of taking care of my pediatric patients, teaching medical students and residents, and nurturing my own son as a single mother didn't leave me much time to practice. I wasn't aware how much of an impact mindfulness would have on my life in the months to follow.

Although it was challenging, I managed to set aside enough time to begin building a personal mindfulness practice, initially for the purpose of managing my high blood pressure. And this gave me the space I needed to see how out of balance my life had become. In the beginning I didn't see much of a difference in my day-to-day life, but over time I noticed that I was more present with my patients in the office. I became aware of increased feelings of compassion both for the people I cared most about in my life and for total strangers. I was also more patient with my son, and I noticed that he was arguing less and that we were communicating more effectively. However, I still had a ways to go in my journey toward mindfulness.

Physician, Heal Thyself

As my awareness increased with my personal mindfulness practice, I realized that I wasn't managing my stress very well.

On an intellectual level I understood what I needed to do to lessen the negative effects of chronic stress on my health, but I was unable to successfully translate this knowledge into action. My ineffective stress management not only affected my life but also had an indirect impact on my son. I noticed that I was less patient with him as my stress increased. At times such as these I often focused on the undesirable behaviors that I saw in him instead of exploring the underlying reasons for the behavior. A child is very good at picking up on subtle cues from a parent and can sense when something is wrong. I soon realized that much of my son's acting out resulted from this sense of anxiety that he was picking up from me. Knowing that I was not being the best parent I could be was upsetting to me, so I used my frustration to motivate myself to deepen my practice. The process seemed simple, but as life got in the way it wasn't always easy. I had to make working on healthy stress management a priority in my busy life. My commitment to the practice helped to sustain me through the challenging times, and the results were amazing.

AN ORIENTATION: MBSR FOR PARENTS AND KIDS

As the years passed, I realized that I had something more that I could offer to my patients and their parents who were experiencing stress—a remedy not found behind the pharmacy counter. I began to introduce families in my practice to mindfulness-based skills as a healthier alternative to managing the stress in their lives.

What Is MBSR?

Mindfulness-based stress reduction (MBSR) was origi-
nated by Jon Kabat-Zinn at the Stress Reduction Clinic at the
University of Massachusetts in 1979. The program is an eight-
week intensive training that meets weekly for ninety-minute
sessions consisting of mindfulness meditation, mindful eating,
and gentle yoga practices. The interactive classes and home
assignments are designed to help participants develop a personal mindfulness practice and awaken to the internal resources
within each of us that will allow us to lead a more present life.

MBSR has been used as a complementary therapy to
manage a number of stress-related conditions and to promote
a greater sense of health and well-being. Specific benefits of
practice include reductions in physical and emotional pain,
improved cardiovascular health, increased energy, greater ability
to relax, and increased feelings of general well-being. Graduates
of MBSR programs have reported more joy, greater enthusiasm
for life, and an improved ability to effectively cope with stress.

MBSR classes are now offered in more than two hundred
medical centers, hospitals, and clinics around the world. Adults
who have participated in MBSR programs often comment that
these skills would have been most helpful had they been introduced to them earlier in life. Be sure to see the Resources
section at the end of this book for information on finding an
MBSR program near you.

Kids Can Be Mindful, Too

Traditionally designed for adults, mindfulness interventions
and MBSR classes are now being adapted for children. Kids

from preschool age up through adolescence are learning about mindfulness and developing skills that they can incorporate into their daily lives (Black, Milam, and Sussman 2009; Wall 2005). Early research findings have demonstrated significant benefits to children who learn mindfulness, including increased resilience, better ability to focus, and a greater sense of well-being (Flook et al. 2010; Garrison Institute 2005).

Given my positive experience with mindfulness practices as a patient and as a parent, I decided to explore the impact of mindfulness as a healthy coping tool for families. During routine office visits I would check in with parents about the stresses they were dealing with. I then asked the child to tell me about her worries, and I asked for permission to teach both parents and child a method to help lessen these worries.

The exercises I taught usually focused on bringing the attention into the present moment using the breath. The following exercise is an example of a brief mindfulness practice that you can easily teach your child to use in any stressful environment.

CHILD EXERCISE: Brief Breath Awareness

1. Find a position that is comfortable for you. You can close your eyes or leave them open, whichever you prefer.

2. Take a moment to notice your breathing. You don't have to change anything about it; just pay attention to each breath as the air moves in and out.

3. Now that you're aware of your breathing, notice the moment in your breathing pattern where the air

stops moving; you may find the pause at the end of the in-breath, or at the end of the out-breath.

4. Spend some time just watching your breath with your mind's eye. If your mind starts to wander, it's okay; gently return your attention to your breathing again.

5. After two to three minutes, return your attention to the room. What did you notice? How does your body feel now compared to the way it felt before you started this exercise?

As a parent, you can practice this exercise yourself and see what you notice. You may find that your body begins to relax and release tension that you didn't even know you were holding on to. Teach your child these stress management skills by going through the above exercise with her. You may want to consider recording the above script so she can listen to it and practice on her own. Remember to talk about the process with her afterward to see what she noticed. Assist her in the process of discovering valuable insights as she becomes more aware of her thoughts and feelings in the present moment.

In office visits, I continued to focus on awareness of breathing in addition to relaxation exercises (see chapters 3 and 4 for specific details on performing these exercises). I recommended journaling as a tool to document and record the insights that came from paying attention to thoughts, emotions, and behaviors. Children took to these practices easily. I discovered that mindfulness practices helped to calm kids before vaccines were given. Children used these new skills in the classroom when they were feeling fearful and at night before bed to help promote sleep. Through mindfulness practices, these kids learned that, while we don't always have control over the events that occur in our lives, we do have a choice in how we respond to them. The awareness cultivated by mindfulness practices disrupts the automatic response to stressful events and situations and creates space to allow a more conscious choice to be made.

The Value of Parents as Role Models

This book will help you to teach your child mindfulness-based skills for stress reduction and healthy coping. You will also learn how to model mindfulness-based skills for your child and find opportunities to remind her to use her breath to calm down and return her attention to the present moment.

Parents serve as primary role models for kids during the early years. Finding positive and healthy ways to cope with the stress in your life will not only help you but also indirectly teach your child about stress management. Practicing mindfulness yourself will help you develop the skills you need for better stress management.

I strongly encourage you to participate in a mindfulness program with your child. When you understand the key concepts of mindfulness and begin to practice them regularly, you may find that the way you respond to stressful events in your life improves. Children learn by observation, and parents can serve as positive role models. Having a regular practice can also allow parents to reinforce the concepts that children are learning and help put the principles into practice throughout the day. You'll find it easier to separate your child's behavior from your child as a person (in other words, "She's not a bad girl; she's just displaying bad behavior") and help her to discern this difference for herself. One of the greatest gifts that may result from your own personal mindfulness practice as a parent is that you can help your child see herself in a positive light through your eyes.

TEN MINDFUL PRACTICES

The strategies within this book can help provide insight for you as you guide your child toward young adulthood. They will assist you in teaching your child how to cope with the daily stress she encounters.

The ten mindful practices in this book provide memorable stories and sample exercises that you can use to teach your child how to fully experience the positive and negative events of life in a healthier way. There are also exercises to help you to better manage your own frustration when your child is stressed. The mindful practices are:

1. **Awareness of Breathing.** There is so much information in the breath. Our breathing becomes rapid and shallow when we are fearful and anxious. It may sometimes feel as though you're holding your breath when you're worried, waiting to exhale with relief when you sense things are safe. Being aware of your breathing develops your ability to return to the present moment by using your breath as an anchor. This practice is recommended for both children and parents.

2. **Relaxation Breathing.** Designed to facilitate release of tension by triggering the relaxation response, this practice is used to promote a sense of calm. Children and parents may both use this skill to quiet anxiety during stressful situations or to prepare for sleep at the end of a long day.

3. **Mindful Walking.** Waking up to the strength of your body as it transports you from place to place throughout your day is a great way to practice being present and connect with your body. You will find multiple opportunities for you and your child to use this practice on a regular basis in the classroom, at work, or at home.

4. **Mindful Movement with Yoga.** Gentle yoga stretches tied to breathing techniques teach your child how to unite the body and mind in the present moment. The result is an increased awareness of the amazing power of the body as your child discovers its flexibility, strength, and ability to relax with regular practice.

5. **Mindful Eating.** This life-sustaining daily habit of nourishing the body is often taken for granted. We often eat on the go or while doing other things without paying attention to the taste of our food or our hunger and satiety cues. This practice will help you and your child to fully experience the joy of eating.

6. **Progressive Muscle Relaxation.** The exercises for this practice will teach your child how to check in with her body and hear the messages that are being

communicated to her all the time. You will learn how to guide her through an exploration of her body to identify which areas hold tension when she is stressed and help her discover how to release it. This practice can help with tension headaches and other physical pain resulting from stress.

7. **Visualization.** Also known as guided imagery, this process stimulates your child's creative side, teaching her how to connect mind and body through exploration of the five senses. This practice is often easy for children to do because it involves an active and vivid imagination, something that comes naturally to most kids.

8. **A Mindful Mind.** Exercises and stories here uncover the busyness of the mind and show you and your child a kinder and gentler way to watch your thoughts as they emerge. Being thankful for what you learn as you each notice your thoughts, you'll begin to let go of the resistance that may accompany negative thoughts and become more accepting of the reality of the present moment.

9. **Loving-Kindness.** So much of our stress comes from our own negative self-talk; we're often our own worst critic. This practice will guide you and your child through an exercise of being kind to yourself and to others. You'll find that your child will likely develop a greater sense of confidence. You may also find that you are gentler with yourself and your child as you cultivate feelings of caring and compassion for yourself, an added benefit for most parents.

10. **The Art of Appreciation.** With this final practice, you will teach your child how to shift from dissatisfaction with what she doesn't have to gratitude for all that she does have right here and now. I encourage you to adopt this practice with your child. This is one of the most valuable gifts for you and your child. You will become genuinely aware of how fortunate you are to have your life, your health, and each other.

Think of the mindful practices as tools in your toolbox. Each practice addresses a specific area in our lives and moves us closer to a path of mindful living from day to day. In working through the mindful practice principles and exercises and practically applying them in everyday situations, you will find that you and your child begin to reap the benefits of developing a mindfulness practice: you will begin to skillfully move yourself to a safer place when life's stresses push you toward the cliff's edge. With regular practice, the interval between the recognition of your emotional state and your decision to take action in a healthy way will gradually decrease, leaving you with a sense of knowing that all is well even when chaos surrounds you.

As you become calmer, you will start to notice these patterns in your child and artfully guide her through the process of safely reducing her stress. Equally rewarding will be the indirect benefits that your child will reap as you model healthy coping strategies. Point out to your child the times when she successfully uses the mindful practice skills to redirect her behavior in response to stressful thoughts and emotions. In this way she can begin to see how using the skills she's learned can make a difference in how she feels and responds to stressful situations.

The "Awareness of Breathing" and "Relaxation Breathing" exercises may help children who struggle with separation anxiety or become nervous before an exam. They may also help her remember to take a breath before impulsively hitting another child out of anger or frustration during tense moments on the playground, for example—that breath can provide the space she needs to make a different choice.

Practice scenarios at home with your child. She will gradually feel more comfortable using the skills if she understands that they can make a difference during difficult situations in her life. One example would be a situation where your child feels she is being treated unfairly by another child. Let's say that your child and two other children are jumping rope on the playground. They are rotating positions so that two children turn the rope while the third child jumps. It's your child's turn to jump, but the other children insist it is not her turn. Talk with your child to discover ways she can use her new mindfulness skills in such a situation. Your discussion may go something like this:

Mother: How do you feel right now?

Child: It's not fair! I know it's my turn!

Mother: It sounds like you're angry because you think they're going to skip your turn.

Child: Yes. If they're not going to play fair, I don't want to play.

Mother: When I'm upset, it sometimes helps for me to take a breath. Let me show you how it works. Close your eyes and take a breath. Let's count the breaths until we get up to ten. Ready? One, two, three *(Continues to count.)*...ten. How do you feel now? Do you still feel angry?

Child: No, not right now.

Mother: What if they didn't skip you on purpose? What if they made a mistake? Or, what if you got confused when you were counting and it really isn't your turn?

Child: I guess they could have made a mistake. I forget sometimes too. Maybe it isn't my turn now.

Mother: What could you do differently if you thought they made a mistake?

Child: Maybe I could tell them it's my turn next and they'd let me jump.

Several key things happened in the scenario above. First, you validated that you heard what your daughter was thinking: she was being treated unfairly. Second, you helped her name the emotion that she was feeling: she felt angry in response to her thought that she was being treated in an unjust way. Her automatic response was to withdraw and say "I don't want to play with them anymore," even though you know jumping rope is one of her favorite activities. Her withdrawal was likely an attempt to avoid getting hurt again. When she stopped to focus on her breathing, the feelings of anger were allowed to dissipate a bit. She could then reexamine her thought process to see if what she perceived was really true or if there could be another reality (in other words, maybe she lost track of whose turn it was). This gave her just enough space to make a different choice, one where she could still play her favorite game without feeling that the other kids were intentionally trying to cheat her out of a turn.

It is so important for parents to show children the connection between thoughts, emotions, and behaviors. Our thoughts are generally neutral. The distress sometimes results when we assign a positive or negative value to what we think about the thought that we are having. In this example, the thought was "I'm going to lose my turn." The child assigned a negative value to this thought when she assumed that the thought was correct and that she had been cheated out of her turn on purpose. Her thinking about this led to an emotion—in this case, anger resulting from feelings of injustice. Her initial response to the feelings could have resulted in her walking away from the game (reactive behavior).

Thoughts are what we hear our mind saying inside our head. Our tendency is to judge thoughts and label them "good" or "bad." The way in which we label thoughts usually generates emotions. Typically the thoughts we think are "good" lead to positive emotions (for example, joy); the thoughts we think are "bad" lead to negative emotions (for example, sadness). The feelings associated with the emotions are what often drive our behaviors. The consequences of our behaviors lead to additional thoughts that trigger more emotions, and the cycle goes on and on.

Mindfulness practices help raise our awareness of our thought process and how we're feeling. As we're brought into the present moment, this creates space that allows us to make a different choice.

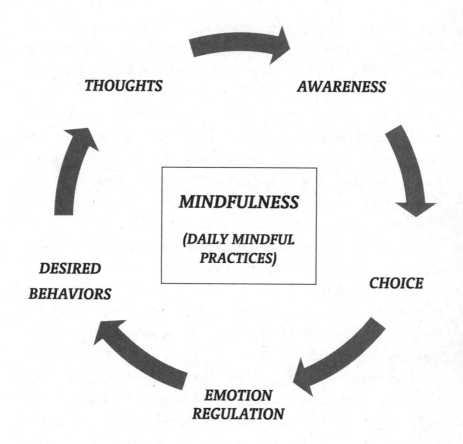

Without the space between our thoughts, feelings, and behaviors, we often feel as though we have no choice regarding how to react. Living in the present moment gives you back your choice. The awareness cultivated through mindful attention helps to improve regulation of emotions, leading to an increase in desired behaviors. We will come back to this important concept over and over again throughout the book.

With your child, review situations in which undesirable behaviors resulted and see if you can identify the points where a choice could have been made. Role-play different scenarios where you know your child may be more likely to experience stress. Examples may include arts or sports performances, transitions to a new school or classroom, or an important test. Even trips to the doctor's office can trigger significant stress for many kids, who may be worried about whether they will get a shot, have to undress, or have to deal with other uncomfortable situations.

I'm certain that you will find this book to be a valuable resource as you help your child build healthy coping strategies for life—a reference that you will reach for regularly.

HOW TO USE THIS BOOK

The introduction and chapters 1 and 2 provide a foundation for understanding how stress has become pervasive in our society and how mindfulness practice offers one path to manage it. You will become more aware of the important role you play in modeling healthy coping strategies for your child—both when she's watching and when you think she's not. This early section of the book (part I) outlines the numerous factors that result in stress and anxiety in the lives of parents and children today. The subjective nature of stress and our perceptions of events that create our reality are also explored here. Mindfulness and MBSR are defined, and the relationship between stress and health is discussed. You will come to understand the specific effects that stress can have on multiple systems throughout the body and the negative consequences of doing nothing to abate it.

Chapters 3 through 12 present the ten mindful practices. Each chapter shares a story that illustrates the core principles of the practice, provides an example of how the practice is used in real life by parents and children, and provides guidance for teaching the practice to your child. Chapter 13 ties all the information together and explains how to incorporate these practices into your child's daily life. At the end of the book are resources that you can consult if you would like to learn more about mindfulness practice for you and your child.

When beginning to learn a new concept, we may have a natural tendency to believe that we fully understand the material that's been presented and that we will be able to incorporate the principles into our life fairly easily. However, knowing information and translating that information into action in your life are two very different things. Although this book provides examples and exercises to teach the principles of mindfulness, mastery comes from a consistent daily practice.

A journal may serve as a valuable tool to help your child keep track of insights gained as you work through the mindful practices. Journals come in many different forms, from paper notebooks, both lined and unlined, to electronic journals. Some children enjoy the process of writing, while others may be more inclined to capture thoughts in the form of pictures or symbols. Either way is fine, as long as you establish a system to document what she is learning along the way. Encourage your child to write something in her journal every day. Set aside ten minutes at the start or end of the day. Developing this habit early in life promotes regular self-reflection, a practice necessary for meaningful personal growth and development.

As you develop your own practice, you will find it easier to see opportunities to use the principles regularly, and you will be able to impart this knowledge to your child. Come back to the exercises over and over again. Find new ways to expand upon them. There is wisdom in the practice. This book will serve as a guide, empowering you to support your child's personal growth and promote inner resilience. Remember to be gentle with yourself and your child as you begin this new journey.

1

Understanding Stress and the Mind-Body Connection

There is no question that the things we think have
a tremendous effect on our bodies. If we change
our thinking, the body frequently heals itself.

—C. Everett Koop, MD, Former Surgeon
General of the United States

Our thoughts create our reality. Much of the stress we feel does not come from the life event or situation that occurs but instead results from what we make the event mean to us. It is our experience of life that translates into our joys and sorrows. The way we think about something and the value we assign to it (positive or negative) affects our mind, and that ultimately has an impact on the physical body. Let's take a look at how the mind and body are connected and how stress can affect that connection.

STRESS IN KIDS IS ON THE RISE

Stress is a part of life. It affects each of us and at every stage of life. While most people acknowledge that stress affects adults, many are unaware of the stress experienced by children on a daily basis. Movies and television programming display provocative images, prematurely exposing children to inappropriate sexual content. Video games, computers, cell phones, television, and extracurricular activities provide a myriad of options to occupy our kids' time. Overscheduled days and continuous stimulation place an incredible amount of stress and pressure on our kids.

Stress has been generally thought to be rare in childhood, but many studies are finding that kids experience moderate to extreme levels of stress in everyday life (American Psychological Association 2007). Pressure to do well in school, peer relationships, and family financial concerns are among several issues that serve as sources of stress for children.

Keep the Lines of Communication Open

If you are like most parents, you probably feel that by keeping your own worries from your child you're shielding him from stress; however, in talking to children in my practice, I find that the opposite is often true. Kids sense when their parents are worried. Children often accidentally overhear discussions about financial difficulties where parents are talking about how they are going to pay the bills this month, for example. And when your child doesn't know what is going on, he may be more likely to fill in the details—perhaps erroneously—on his own. This can lead to feelings of anxiety or self-blame for what's perceived as a parent's distress.

Instead of unintentionally adding to your child's stress by keeping information hidden, share with him what's going on. He doesn't require many details—just enough to reassure him that he is safe and secure. Providing general information about the events affecting your family and talking to your child about your own feelings that result from stress is a good first step in beginning the dialogue. You might start the discussion like this:

Dad: You may have noticed that I've been working a lot more lately. I know I haven't been around as much, and I'm tired and a little grumpier when I get home. I worry sometimes that I don't have enough money to give you everything that you want. I just wanted you to know that I'm working hard to make sure I can provide the things that we need—a safe place to live and enough food to eat. I miss spending time with you. Things are a little hard right now but I know they will get better. What kinds of things do you worry about?

Then listen to what he has to say. Communicating honestly about your concerns and worries demonstrates the importance of talking about what's bothering you. Be patient if your child doesn't have anything to share initially. With time and proper role modeling, he will understand that it is safe to talk about his worries and the feelings surrounding them. Remember that he will be watching you, looking for signs of reassurance that all is well. Learning to cope with the stress in your life in a healthy way builds confidence in your child that he can do the same. Despite what we may like to believe, kids place a greater emphasis on what we do than on what we say.

An Everyday Occurrence

Certain routine occurrences can cause stress for most people. You may or may not have noticed these things but, over time, they can take their toll on your health and well-being. Examples of such daily stressors for parents include commuting in heavy traffic or for long distances, getting the kids ready for school on time, and putting dinner on the table every evening.

Your child has stress throughout his day too. Making a transition, whether it's to a new school, a new teacher, or a new grade, can be stressful. He may worry that he will be called on in class and not know the right answer. He might feel out of place on the playground because he doesn't run as fast as the other boys or doesn't do as well in sports. He may be teased about the clothes he wears or the way he wears his hair. Or, if he is like my son, he may wonder if he will be the last child picked up from the after-school program, again!

These and other issues are very real sources of stress for your child. Young children do not yet have a strong sense of self. As a result, a child can be easily influenced by the perceptions of other people, such as parents, teachers, and peers. To make matters worse, children often do not have the verbal skills to adequately articulate feelings and emotions. As a result, your child may act out, displaying disruptive behavior or withdrawing and isolating from friends and family.

The way in which kids display stress varies considerably depending on the age and maturity of the child. For some children, stress hurts—manifesting itself as physical symptoms such as headaches, chest pain, or tummy aches. For others, fluctuations in emotional states may occur as mood swings, irritability, or the development of significant fears. Still other children will withdraw and isolate themselves, suffering in silence.

CHILD EXERCISE: How Does Your Child Respond to Stress?

1. Ask your child, "What do you worry about?" Wait for an answer.

2. Using a journal or small notebook, make a list of the things that cause stress for your child. Find out how he handles the worry. You may ask, "What do you do to make yourself feel better when you're worried?" Write down what he says. This is one of your child's current stress management strategies.

3. Once you've created the list of stressors and discussed the coping strategies, ask him to select the item that causes the greatest worry. Next, ask him to describe how he feels when he's worried about this situation. (If your child is unable to identify what he's feeling, review the sample dialogue regarding a playground conflict on page 20, and adapt that discussion to the current situation; this way, you will be able to help guide him to identify his feelings.) Write the feelings next to the item on the list. For example, if he says he worries when you're late getting home, he may feel scared, angry, and/or sad. It's okay if more than one emotion emerges for a given situation—this is natural.

4. Now help him to explore what thoughts may trigger the feelings of sadness, anger, and/or fear. You may learn that he thinks you have been hurt in a car accident, or he may think that you're angry with him because he got into trouble last night and that you don't want to come home because of him. Work through each of the thoughts that may contribute to the corresponding emotion.

Explain that we all have different ways to deal with the stress in our life. Some ways are healthy and others are not. Breathing is one way to help positively shift your body toward relaxation when it is in overdrive.

Once you have completed the stress assessment exercise above, guide your child through the following relaxation breath exercise. These instructions are geared toward your child, but I encourage you to try it with him.

CHILD EXERCISE:
Blow Away Your Stress

1. Sit in a comfortable position in a chair or on the floor. If your child has any nasal congestion, ask him to blow his nose (or blow your own, if you need to) prior to starting this exercise. You will need to breathe through your nose in this exercise, so clearing the nasal passages will be helpful.

2. Gently place the tip of your tongue behind your two front teeth and let it stay there for the entire exercise.

3. Exhale completely through your mouth, around your tongue, making a blowing sound.

4. Close your mouth and inhale quietly through your nose while counting to four inside your head. For younger children, it may be helpful to use fingers for counting in this exercise.

5. Hold your breath for a count of seven.

6. Exhale completely through your mouth, making a blowing sound, to a count of eight. This concludes one breath cycle. Repeat for a total of four breath cycles.

This breath, also known as the "four-seven-eight breath," is designed to promote feelings of calm by triggering the parasympathetic nervous system, which leads to relaxation. Practice this breath exercise twice a day. In the beginning, do not do more than four breath cycles at once. With regular practice, you may work your way up to eight breath cycles after about thirty days. It is common to experience some lightheadedness in the beginning. This is normal and will pass. Encourage your child to use this breath practice when he is feeling stressed or worried.

All Stressors Are Not Created Equal

Stress is subjective. The same event may have very little effect on one person but a significant impact on another. Your child encounters stressful situations on a daily basis, such as deciding what to wear to school, being called on in class, or not having his favorite "lucky" pen when taking an exam. You may read these examples and think that the concerns are inconsequential, but to your child they may loom large in the context of his day. In addition to these "minor" stresses, there are also major stresses and traumas that can change our lives in dramatic ways. A divorce, the death of a loved one, and natural disasters are all major life events that change the way that children look at the world. In the face of such a major life event, a youngster feels vulnerable as his day-to-day life becomes unstable. Kids who worry regularly, whether from seemingly minor stresses or from major traumatic events, are at much greater risk for physical symptoms of stress.

It's important to remember that the same situation may produce very little stress for one child, significant stress for another, and no stress at all for yet another. The reaction depends upon the age, personality, and emotional resiliency of the child. An event that you think may cause stress for your child may have the opposite effect. Similarly, a situation that you anticipate being enjoyable for your child may cause a great deal of stress. This was the case when I hired a clown for my son's fifth birthday party. His reaction was one of fear, which I had not anticipated. After the clown arrived, I noticed that my son became very clingy and seemed sad. Instead of having fun while the clown performed for his friends, my son retreated to the safety of my arms, not wanting to go near the clown or have the clown come too close to him.

Each child may display a range of symptoms when under stress. So how would you know if your child were demonstrating signs of stress? Table 1 lists common signs and symptoms that kids in middle childhood (five to twelve years old) may exhibit when they are stressed.

TABLE 1. Signs and Symptoms of Stress in Middle Childhood

Physical reactions	Headaches
	Neck pain/stiffness
	Chest pain/rapid heartbeat
	Stomachaches
	Nausea/vomiting
	Diarrhea/constipation
	Fatigue
Change in lifestyle habits	Decrease or increase in appetite
	Sleep disturbances (such as bad dreams, difficulty falling asleep or staying asleep, and increased sleep)
	Poor school performance
	Less concern about appearance
	Changes in physical activity habits (such as increased or decreased exercise and/or sports participation)
Emotional reactions	Tension
	Irritability/short temper
	Pervasive sadness
	Unpredictable changes in mood
	Loneliness
Behavioral reactions	Aggression
	Separation anxiety
	Difficulty focusing
	Withdrawal and isolation from friends and/or family
	Lying
	Stealing

Whether major or minor, stress wreaks havoc on our sense of calm and well-being. Much of the distress is a direct reflection of our thoughts. The way we think about an event, a person, or our self is what leads to the negative emotions that cause us to feel bad. Kids are susceptible to this type of thought pattern, but they are often unable to name the emotion and are unaware of the thoughts that triggered the emotion. Being unaware of the relationship between our thoughts, feelings, and behavior is disempowering for both adults and children—and it may lead your child to believe that he has no control over his own behavior. You may forget about the connection between thoughts, feelings, and behaviors as well, confusing his behavior with him as a person.

When you find your child automatically reacting to a stressful situation, you both need to pause and interrupt the cycle in order to get control again. The following three-step process can help to manage emotions through the stress.

CHILD EXERCISE: Calm Down— Deep Breath—Thought Mirror

1. Gently remind your child to pause in order to allow his body to calm down. This is the first step in taking a time-out before climbing the ladder of stress.

2. Have your child take a deep breath to break the cycle of hormones triggered by the stress response and help him to feel less anxious and stressed in the moment.

3. Once your child is calmer, he can stop to take a look at the thoughts that were triggered by the stressful situation. Ask him to imagine holding up a mirror to look at the thoughts he's having; this is a kinder way to explore and reflect on how we sometimes create more stress and anxiety for ourselves. This step also provides some space for him to make a different choice. Ask him, "Is the thought true?" If the answer is yes, ask him how he knows it's true. How would he feel if it weren't true? What would he do differently? This is the beginning of a process of awareness that is truly empowering for your child as he learns how to face life's challenges rather than impulsively reacting to them.

With regular practice, your child will find he's able to develop an effective strategy for handling minor stresses, major stresses, and everything in between. We will revisit this important concept again throughout the book.

THE MIND-BODY CONNECTION

For most children, the body and the mind are so closely connected that they are indistinguishable. However, as our lives have become busier, a growing estrangement between the body and the mind seems to have developed, both for adults and for children. The result is that we (children and adults alike) are losing touch with our feelings. We stuff our emotions like we are packing a suitcase for a long vacation. What is the danger in not allowing ourselves to feel? Well, the emotions will show up later, in undesirable ways that generally have a negative impact on our physical and emotional health and well-being. Sometimes our stuffed feelings will seep out in the form of physical pain. Tension headaches, chest pain, and abdominal pain are a few examples. The pain is real, but we may ignore the underlying cause for fear of unleashing issues that we do not yet feel ready to face. At other times it will affect our behavior. Aggression, conflict, and other negative states are usually associated with hidden emotions.

Your body responds to the way you think, feel, and act. You experience this connection whether you are aware of it or not. The body is always in the present moment, taking us here and there throughout our day. It is our mind that often drifts back into the past or forward into the future, very seldom settling in to the here and now. This is true with parents and kids. So what's the solution? Bringing the mind into alignment with the body in the present moment raises our conscious awareness of our thoughts and feelings and helps us to better understand our actions. Once we are aware of the factors that underlie our behavior, we are in a position to make a different choice if we are unhappy with the results of our current circumstances.

Understanding the wisdom of the connection between our mind and body is a key first step toward achieving peace of mind. Mindfulness can help you cultivate present moment awareness to reconnect the mind and the body, enabling you to honestly face the challenges that bring stress into your life. Practicing the principles of mindfulness will equip you with the knowledge that you need in order to teach healthy coping skills to your child, ensuring a healthier emotional future.

The Effect of Emotions on the Physical Body

"Mommy, I don't feel good." Many parents have heard these words. You feel the forehead to check for fever. You ask your child where it hurts. You investigate to find a clue that will reveal what may be going on with your little one. The headache or tummy ache that your child is experiencing in the moment is very real to him. But dig a little deeper and you may learn that today is the day that he has to stand in front of the class and read an excerpt from the book that has too many big words. Or perhaps tonight is the martial arts test that he has been dreading.

Our emotional state is largely determined by our thoughts. The boy who is afraid of reading to the class may be thinking, "I'll say a word wrong and everyone will laugh at me. They'll all think I'm stupid." The boy who is fearful of performing solo may have thoughts like "What if I trip and fall? What happens if I don't remember all the movements? Mr. Johnson won't like me anymore and I won't ever want to practice again." When thoughts such as these spin out of control, children feel a sense of fear and anxiety. The mind doesn't differentiate between a real threat (such as a vicious dog charging toward you) and a perceived threat (such as the possibility that you will get in trouble for being late). The effect on the body is the same once the cascade of stress hormones is initiated, which the body produces in order to prepare you to "fight" or "flee." A flood of symptoms is unleashed—including feelings of butterflies in the stomach, rapid breathing, and a heart pounding so hard it seems that it will crash through your chest at any moment.

Some stress, in some circumstances, can be advantageous, for example when it helps you to perform better. However, too much stress can have the opposite effect, causing you significant emotional or physical distress. The stress in each of the examples mentioned above was intensified by the thoughts about the situation. It's the way we think about an event and what we make it mean to us (or about us) that leads to negative emotions and causes us to feel bad. Kids often overlook the thought but rather pay attention to the negative feelings that result. Similarly, as an adult you may not be aware of the primary thoughts that triggered the emotion in your child. Instead, you focus in on the child's behavior. This disconnection is disempowering, because it leads you and your child to believe that he does not have any control over his own behavior. If, however, you can get your child to use the three-step "Calm Down— Deep Breath—Thought Mirror" process described earlier in the chapter, he may begin to understand why he's feeling so upset.

This process of self-reflection helps him to explore his thoughts and feelings in greater detail. Using the mind-body connection, he may then begin to use the skills he's learning to bring about a sense of relaxation and calm in the midst of emotional chaos. Once you and your child begin to see how thinking influences our mood and feelings, it will be easier for your child to change his experience by altering the way he views his thoughts.

The Good, the Bad, and the Ugly

Pain and suffering are two terms that are often used together. We have come to think of these words as synonymous; however, that couldn't be further from the truth. Pain resulting from physical or emotional wounds feels bad, but suffering encompasses so much more. Suffering may be defined as the despair that results from feeling a lack of control over your circumstances and your life. Children sometimes feel this way, acquiescing to the desires and commands of the adults who care for them. So, as you can see, it is possible to experience pain without suffering and to have suffering without physical pain.

The bad news is that we sometimes allow the mind to create a harsh reality made up of negative thoughts, resulting in an inner world full of hopelessness and despair. Let's take a look at Carl's story.

> *Carl is a bright eight-year-old boy. He excels in school and adores his third-grade teacher, Ms. Bell. Carl enjoys receiving praise from Ms. Bell when he answers her questions correctly.*
>
> *One day he raised his hand to answer every question she asked, but Ms. Bell didn't call on him even once. He didn't understand—she usually called on him. "She didn't call on me. She doesn't like me anymore," Carl thought. Carl's feelings were hurt, and he went home and cried after school. After that day, Carl didn't raise his hand in class anymore. He gradually stopped paying attention in class and by the middle of the term his grades had fallen from As to Cs. When Ms. Bell asked him why he was doing so poorly in her class he remained silent. He never told anyone about that day—not his parents and not Ms. Bell.*

The original thought that Carl had was neutral: Ms. Bell didn't call on him in class that day. But he interpreted this thought in a negative way: "She doesn't like me anymore." His interpretation caused him to feel sad and hurt, and he reacted to these emotions by withdrawing from his teacher and not participating in class. In reality, Ms. Bell didn't call on Carl that day in order to allow other children to respond to questions. She knew Carl was one of her brightest students and she wanted to encourage other kids who seldom spoke up in class. Ms. Bell was confused by Carl's subsequent difficulty in her class, but she assumed that Carl's grades had dropped because the work had grown harder.

Carl's mother, a single parent who works two jobs to make ends meet, has always been proud of her son's academic gifts, and she was concerned when he started having trouble in school. After meeting with his teacher she began to worry that maybe Carl had attention deficit disorder (ADD), or maybe Carl's grades were suffering because she wasn't home as often as she wanted to be. She felt guilty about having to work so much. She found a tutor to help him with his schoolwork at the local community center. When the tutoring didn't help, she scheduled an appointment with his pediatrician to discuss testing for ADD.

Carl had gotten caught in the thought-emotion-behavior cycle. Without the words to clearly articulate his thoughts or the skill to effectively cope with his negative feelings, Carl entered a downward spiral. This kind of interior world is a virtual reality full of endless perceived threats that can fuel chronic stress in your child's life. The picture painted here was a bleak one for Carl, leading to feelings of sadness and loneliness. So how do you help your child to break free of this cycle?

The secret is in knowing that although the mind can paint a negative picture, it can also create a more positive reality. Learning to foster positive thoughts in addition to simply accepting the existence of the negative ones can help your child to build a kinder and more nurturing world for himself. Understanding how the mind can be either friend or foe is a key step toward learning to harness the power of the mind.

As we have seen, the mind can trigger the stress response when it perceives a threat. The good news is that it can also trigger the relaxation response and produce the opposite effect. Mindfulness is one way to help your child free his mind from suffering. How can using mindfulness accomplish this? Mindfulness increases awareness by teaching your child how to improve his attention in the present moment. Much of suffering occurs when you allow yourself to be drawn into the past or pushed into the future, when you worry about events from the past that cannot be changed, or when you create stories about the future that have not yet happened. Mindfulness shows you how to bring your attention to the present moment, face the reality of what is happening now, and be gentle with yourself as you respond (rather than react) to the current situation.

One sure way to always return your attention to the present during moments of stress is to focus on the breath.

EXERCISE: Noticing the Breath

Imagine that you've just put breakfast on the table and your child has begun to eat. You've timed everything perfectly and know that you need to leave the house in fifteen minutes to drop your child off at school and get yourself to work on time. Suddenly you hear "Uh-oh!" You turn around to find your child's entire glass of milk spilled across the table and quickly pooling on the floor. What do you do? There are numerous ways that this scenario could play out. As the parent in this situation, you may find that practicing mindfulness in the moment can help to reduce the stress that this situation may cause.

For the Parent

Stop for a moment to pay attention to your breathing. You may be breathing rapidly and notice that you're feeling a bit tense. Don't judge yourself; you're just noticing. Over the next thirty to sixty seconds you're likely to realize that your breathing rate is slowing down and the tension is easing out of your neck and shoulders. This brief pause creates space for you to decide what you want to do about this situation. You may be able to reassure your child that all is well and enlist his help in cleaning up the mess.

For the Child

Similarly, you can help your child to see this situation from a different perspective. He's probably feeling sad and a bit fearful about what consequences he may face as a result of this situation (in other words, he is worrying about the future). You may say to him, "Let's take a minute to just look at our breathing together." Guide him through this process; point out that he may notice that he's breathing fast or that his heart is pounding. Ask him to pay attention to what he's feeling and the thoughts that are in his head. Then allow him to be silent. At the end of the minute, ask him how he's feeling. What thoughts did he notice?

How do you think your child may react now that he took some time to feel and reflect before reacting? Perhaps he will apologize for the spill and offer to clean it up without having a temper tantrum.

Taking one to three minutes to help you both return to center and curtail the potential escalation of stress is well worth the time. Empowering your child to understand ways in which he does have control of his response to stressful events is an invaluable gift that will last a lifetime.

INNER WISDOM

We are all born with an innate knowledge of what is right for us. Some people call this "intuition," a system of guidance that is found within each individual. More accurately called "inner wisdom," this natural ability is not nurtured often enough in our children or in ourselves. The voice that communicates this knowledge is heard not with your ears but rather with your heart. This soft voice is often not heard over the noise of your life. It speaks whether we're listening or not; whether we choose to hear the whispers is entirely up to us. Listening to our inner wisdom helps us to connect with who we really are and what is best for us. Giving your attention to the inner life, your thoughts and feelings, and checking in with your body, can assist you and your child in hearing the inner voice when it speaks.

How do you cultivate this inner wisdom? Invite silence and stillness into your life. Many families today leave the television on just to have some noise in the environment. The radio or CD player may be the first thing you reach for when you get into the car. So often we avoid silence. But there is so much peace to be found there. Incorporate moments of silence and stillness into your daily life. You may decide to wait five minutes before turning the radio on in the car, or adopt a five-minute rule for turning on the television when you get home. These small steps begin to help you and your child become more comfortable with silence. Gradually lengthen the intervals of silence in your day. You may be surprised to find how many answers to questions you've been asking seem to arise out of nowhere when you allow yourself to spend time in silence.

Teach your child how to do this. Encourage him to take time each day to just be still. Sitting for a few minutes to transition from one activity to another is a great way to practice. Ask him to think about the activity that he just completed. What new information did he learn? How did he feel before, during, and after the activity? He can answer these questions silently as he sits in quiet reflection. Have him pay attention to his breathing for a few breaths. He may notice thoughts that arise as he sits quietly. Some of these thoughts may provide useful information for him. Others may not. Remind him not to judge the thoughts. He's using his mind's eyes and ears to watch and listen to the messages coming up for him in the moment. Teach him to listen for the still, quiet voice within and to trust this inner knowing. The exercises found in this book will help him to develop practices that continue to encourage and support this process of reflective inquiry.

In the film version of L. Frank Baum's *The Wizard of Oz*, Dorothy travels a long distance to find someone who can help her get home, only to be told, "You had the power...all along." We all have this power as well. But we don't need ruby slippers to magically transport us. All we need is to tune in to the innate wisdom that can be found inside. We spend so much time looking for answers outside of ourselves to solve our greatest problems. This gift is always with us if we would just pay attention to it.

Increasing awareness through mindfulness practices will highlight this natural talent in numerous ways. As you begin to pay attention to your thought patterns and emotions, you will find that you learn more about yourself; you'll understand how to listen to the whisperings of your inner wisdom and recognize subtle changes within your body that let you know when you're uncomfortable with an action or behavior. It's like having a built-in GPS device.

CHILD EXERCISE:
Finding Your Heart Songs

Follow the steps below to guide your child through the exercise. This activity is a great way to help your child become comfortable with silence and listen for the voice of innate wisdom that we all have inside. A quiet space is recommended for practicing this exercise.

1. Ask your child to get into a comfortable position in a chair or on the floor and close his eyes when he's ready.

2. Tell him to take a moment to notice his breathing. Say, "You don't have to change anything about it; just pay attention to each breath as the air moves in and out."

3. Next, ask him to picture his heart sitting inside his chest. "Imagine that your heart contains a radio. Your job is to find the station that plays the messages that are clearly for you."

4. Suggest, "In order to hear your messages, you need to listen carefully as you turn the dial. When you

hear a lot of noise or static, you'll know that you're not tuned in to your station yet."

5. Say, "Your messages will come through in the silence." "Be patient and really listen. The voice that you hear clearly in the stillness is bringing messages just for you. These are your heart songs. The songs on your station may help you find the answer to a problem you've been having or point you in the right direction when you need to make a difficult decision."

6. Have your child spend some time just listening to his special station. Let him know that if his mind starts to wander, that's okay, and that he should gently return his attention to his breathing again and then go back to listening.

7. Give your child five to seven minutes to sit in silence. Then ask him what he noticed. What special messages did he hear? How does his body feel now compared to before starting this exercise? How does his mind feel? (For example, he may say that his mind feels quiet.)

The above exercise can help your child to tune in to his life. Asking open-ended questions before starting this exercise can help your child to identify the natural talents and strengths that he has to offer the world. For example, you might ask, "Which of your gifts would you most like to share with the world? What makes your heart sing?"

Mindfulness helps you to know where you are in this moment, and your inner navigational system helps guide you toward your destination, one step at a time. When you listen to your inner wisdom, you'll feel that you're on the right path as you progress along your journey. Cultivate this skill in your child by sharing your own experiences of your inner wisdom as you develop your mindfulness practice. Once you are more connected with your inner life, you will both come to "feel" this knowing and will recognize it as the truth—your truth.

Tapping into an Abundant Resource

What is it that we need in order to support and empower ourselves to live our life to the fullest? A strong inner core, and I'm not talking about abs here. Certainly, the purpose of your physical inner core, the muscles of your trunk and spine, is to keep your body and spine stable while you move. This helps to improve your posture and helps you maintain balance and prevent falls and injury. But you also have an emotional inner core. This core builds your confidence and helps you to feel more secure in your body. It provides stability when life is tumultuous, helping you to quickly restore your balance. Most important, it allows you to embrace the reality of whatever you find as your attention settles into the present moment.

When you want to strengthen your physical inner core, you perform exercises: sit-ups, push-ups, and so on. Here are a few exercises for you and your child to practice to begin to build your emotional inner core:

PARENT EXERCISE:
Listening to Your Inner Voice

1. Find a quiet place to sit. You may choose to be indoors or outdoors.

2. Take a deep breath. Know that you have nowhere else to be and nothing else to do in this moment.

3. Silently ask yourself, "Who am I?" Turn your attention inward to look for the answer. Resist the temptation to use labels that you or others have used to define you (such as "mother," "wife," and others).

4. Imagine that you are meeting yourself for the very first time. How would you describe yourself? Don't answer immediately; wait for the answers to come from within.

5. It's okay if nothing comes to mind; don't force this process. The answers will come in time. Be patient with yourself.

Getting to know yourself beyond the multiple identities you've adopted will help you develop a valuable inner strength and resiliency. Make the time to be still. These periods of quiet reflection and turning your attention inward will help you to rediscover who you truly are.

CHILD EXERCISE:
Discovering Your Inner Beauty

1. This exercise can be practiced indoors or outdoors. Have your child find something that he thinks is beautiful—an object in nature such as a butterfly or plant, or something that he treasures.

2. Have your child gaze upon the object he has selected.

3. Tell him to close his eyes and feel the beauty of this object—not touching it with his hands but experiencing it in his heart and with his spirit. Once he has done this, have him focus his attention inward. Ask him to feel this same beauty within himself. He may have to sit for a few minutes to find it. Reassure him that it is there.

Having your child reflect on his inner beauty helps to build a strong sense of self. With regular practice, your child will come to see himself in a positive way, looking for the beauty within himself instead of focusing on what he perceives as negative aspects of himself.

You can help reinforce this practice by pointing out what makes him beautiful. Highlight his compassion toward others or his natural ability to make people laugh. Turning the spotlight on his gifts and talents helps him to see the beauty in his unique qualities. Catch him in these moments and bring them to his attention, and soon he will be more connected to his inner supply of wisdom—an abundant, infinite source that he will be able to tap into whenever he needs perspective and reassurance.

Tuning in to your life will help you understand your individual tendencies as well. This in turn can help you develop a plan that leaves you feeling more energized and more present at work, school, and home.

BALANCING LIFE

Whether we are children or adults, we are all tasked with learning how to achieve and maintain balance in our lives. As a parent, you will need to manage primary work responsibilities, household chores, extracurricular activities, and the family's finances. Your child will work to juggle schoolwork with extracurricular activities, chores, and spending time with friends. In both cases, this may leave very little time for "self-care." The additional stress of wanting to provide meaningful opportunities to ensure your child's success can lead to a very overscheduled life for both you and your child.

But children also require unscheduled "free time." This time allows for creative play, an important part of healthy development for kids. How can you provide a sense of balance for you and your child that allows for free time, while handling your endless to-do lists, responsibilities, and activities? Build in time to truly connect with one another. Mindful communication is one way to accomplish this. Mindful listening is an active process where you suspend your own thoughts about what you want to say when there is a break in the conversation and instead listen to the person speaking with an open heart. Mindful listening takes some practice. Here's an activity to get you started.

PARENT AND CHILD EXERCISE:
Mindful Listening

1. Sit with your child in a quiet room, removing any obvious distractions (turn off the TV, radio, or any other source of distraction).

2. Tell your child to clap his hands sharply three times (or ring a bell or chime three times if you prefer). He then gets three minutes to tell you about his day, without being interrupted. You are not allowed to ask questions or make comments during this time. While he is speaking listen respectfully to what he is saying without judgment or providing advice. Avoid the temptation to think about what you will say when it's your turn.

3. After three minutes have passed, clap your hands three times and share anything you want your child to know about your day. Ask him to follow the same instructions for listening that you followed in step 2.

4. Once you've both had a chance to speak, share how it felt to really be listened to in this way. Did you feel heard? What did you notice when you were the listener? When you were the speaker? Did your child feel special having you all to himself for this brief period of time?

Your child will appreciate feeling heard when you've listened in this way. This is a great skill to practice during family meals or during bedtime chats with your child. It also sets up the expectation that you will be there to listen when he really needs you—which is especially important for him as your child gets older. In addition, when you are being present with your child and give him your undivided attention, you are modeling for him how to make time for what's important in life. Finally, mindful listening is a great way for you to communicate and connect with what's going on in your child's life while allowing him to build his mindful practice skills. Mindful listening is not only for parents to do with their kids—it's also a powerful exercise for you to try with your partner. If you practice mindful listening regularly, you may find that your communication with your partner improves as well.

Life Is Dynamic

When life seems challenging, you may think to yourself that everything will fall into place once you acquire the new house, are earning a higher salary, or experience some other life-changing event—then your life will be manageable. Your child may fall prey to the same type of thinking—that everything will be better once he moves to the next grade or makes the sports team. We expect life to change in ways that we think will serve us but to remain the same in other ways. What we fail to realize is that life does not wait for everything to be in order from our perspective. It has its own path that we cannot control, just like the ebb and flow of the tide and the phases of the moon.

I was reminded of this fact while sitting in yoga class. As a student new to yoga, I watched the instructor, who had more than twenty years' experience, with admiration as she struck the most beautiful standing pose. She looked so graceful, and it all seemed so effortless. I was encouraged that I too would be able to easily master this apparently simple pose. I stood on my mat, trying to imitate what I'd just seen, expecting to be able to achieve the pose in no time. Instead, I teetered back and forth, unable to find my balance to maintain the pose. Just when I thought I had it, I would suddenly fall to one side. Amid my frustration I heard my instructor gently whisper to me, "Relax into the pose. Work with your body and not against it." She encouraged me to find the rhythm of my body as I focused my attention on the pose. This helped me to feel less defeated when I toppled over, as I continued to work to establish and maintain balance.

After much practice (approximately six months of dedicated practice, in fact) I was finally able to add this to my list of conquered poses, but the lesson I had learned was far more valuable: although it appeared that I was simply standing still, I was actually working very hard to maintain the balance I'd found. It meant shifting my weight forward one moment and leaning ever so slightly to the left the next moment. The pose is dynamic, just like our lives. What helps us to achieve balance on any given day may change like the seasons. If we expect life to remain unchanged, we will continue to be met with disappointment, longing for it to be something that it is not. But if we accept that life brings change, we can meet these challenges, knowing that with a little practice we'll be able to make the adjustments necessary to maintaining our balance.

Learning to Bend with the Winds of Change

Change is a part of life. It requires that we make some transition from one state of being to another. But, whether the change is perceived by the individual as positive or negative, it often brings with it varying degrees of stress. Learning to be flexible when change comes helps us move through the transition smoothly and builds our confidence in our own ability to manage the winds of change. The skills offered in this book will serve as a foundation for emotional health and wellness that your child may build on over a lifetime.

2

Increasing Awareness with Mindfulness

Yesterday is gone. Tomorrow has not yet come.
We have only today. Let us begin.

—Mother Teresa

Stress management is not a new concept. Magazine articles abound with tips and strategies to help you to become better equipped to handle the stress in your life. The self-help section in any bookstore is lined with books that offer guidance for minimizing and even eliminating stress. Time management is often a key component of the strategies suggested.

Having read many of these kinds of articles and books, I can say from personal experience that, while they seemed logical, the tools were difficult to incorporate into my day-to-day life for any sustained period of time. I felt I was able to manage my stress as long as I was between crises. However, when life became busier than usual or an unexpected event was rolled into my path, I, like so many others, resorted to my old habits, too weary and overwhelmed to remember the lines I'd read in that magazine article so many weeks or months ago.

I discovered that, instead of managing time, which can be so elusive, or trying to eliminate stress, which would inevitably come, I needed to manage myself. A change needed to happen that would result in a natural tendency to draw upon the strength that I knew was within me.

MINDFUL STRESS MANAGEMENT 101

Developing a mindfulness practice has allowed me to make that internal shift. How can making this shift help you and your child? Mindfulness helps you to live in the present moment. It pulls you out of the past, where you are more likely to get bogged down by negative thoughts of a time gone by that you are unable to change. And it gently pushes you back to the present during those times when you find you've leapt into the future, flying on the wings of worries or "what-ifs."

When your child is stressed, it may be difficult for her to give voice to her feelings; instead, she may act out by arguing or withdrawing from family activities. It would be understandable for you to become frustrated as you focus on the undesirable behavior. Practicing mindfulness can help you notice your emotions (frustration, helplessness) and your thoughts "I wish she would talk to me about what's really going on") as you deal with this challenging situation. Taking a moment to breathe and check in with yourself about what's going on inside you can help you to consciously respond rather than impulsively react to your child's behavior.

Contributing to your frustration and helplessness is the voice of the critic inside your head that quickly reminds you of all of your shortcomings and mercilessly beats up on your belief in yourself. To make matters worse, your child also hears her own internal critic loudly shouting and pointing out all of the ways she falls short on a daily basis. How do we all learn to replace this harsh voice with a calmer and gentler one?

Loving-kindness meditation, practiced in mindfulness-based stress reduction (MBSR), helps you to cultivate a deep sense of caring and compassion toward yourself and all living creatures. It is the first of a series of meditations that produce four qualities of love: friendliness, compassion, appreciative joy, and equanimity. The practice generally begins with developing a loving acceptance of yourself. The following is an example of a loving-kindness exercise that you can practice with your child:

PARENT AND CHILD EXERCISE: Loving-Kindness Practice

In the first set of statements below, you and your child are asking for positive feeling states for yourselves. Say each phrase aloud, repeating three times:

> May I be happy.
>
> May I be safe.
>
> May I be healthy.
>
> May I be peaceful.

Practice this exercise at least twice daily and as needed throughout the day.

PARENT EXERCISE: Loving-Kindness Practice for a Loved One

The statements that follow refer to your child. You are asking for these positive feeling states for her. Your wish for her is wellness: physical, mental, and spiritual well-being. Say each phrase aloud, repeating three times:

> May she be happy.
>
> May she be safe.

May she be healthy.

May she be peaceful.

Practice this exercise at least twice daily and as needed throughout the day. You may find that you and your child feel more at peace as you go through the day, regardless of the events that occur.

Loving-kindness teaches you how to be gentle with yourself and others when you're tempted to be critical and harsh. The loving-kindness found in mindfulness gives you permission to be kind to yourself, to receive the nurturing and love that you may often give to everyone else but seldom give to yourself.

Regular practice will simplify the way in which you look at the stress that comes your way, and it will also strengthen your belief that, no matter what challenges may come your way along this life journey, you will be okay. These practices can strengthen your bond with your child as you learn to manage your emotions in response to her stress and assist her in developing healthy coping strategies. You will learn more about loving-kindness practice in chapter 11.

One of the primary benefits of developing a mindfulness practice is that it allows you to build a foundation of resiliency for your child and for you as a parent. Learning to live in the present moment more often will help you to more fully experience your life as it is unfolding. The nonjudgmental nature of the practice provides a healthy way for you to examine your mistakes so that you learn from your experiences rather than get bogged down in them. The loving-kindness practices teach you how to forgive yourself and others when you make mistakes and help you to cultivate love for yourself and others. Finally, through these practices, you can better understand your child and the way she manages stress while still seeing her for who she truly is. You will also begin to better understand yourself, so you can develop individual parenting guidelines for yourself— allowing you to become the best parent that you can be while modeling healthy life skills for your child. Practicing mindfulness as a family can bring you together; you will begin to see through the illusions created by negative feelings and instead learn to love, support, and encourage one another through both the good and the challenging times.

As you and your child embark upon this journey together, remember that it is a practice. You won't do it perfectly, and perfection is really not the goal. The more you practice, the more you will remember to use the principles to bring you back to center, back into the present moment.

Let's begin by looking at the process that occurs within the body when you encounter stress and understand how mindfulness practices can truly help you to not only survive the stresses but also thrive along the way.

The Stress Reaction

The body has a physical ability to react to stress. This built-in survival mechanism served us well when we faced life-threatening challenges in ancient times. Today, this system is in overdrive more often than not, responding to the constant pressures and stresses we face on a daily basis. The body responds in a very predictable way when the mind perceives a stressful situation. This process begins when adrenaline and cortisol are released. Together, these chemicals, also known as *stress hormones*, produce an effect on multiple systems within the body. Your heart rate increases to send more blood to the muscles in case you need to run to get out of harm's way. This produces the feeling of your heart pounding out of your chest. You breathe faster to get more oxygen delivered to all of the tissues in the body. The production of blood sugar accelerates, sending a steady stream of fuel to multiple organ systems so they can function optimally, and muscles become tense in order to guard against injury and pain.

Acute stress is generally short-lived and presents itself during a brief but intense challenge to the body, such as during a school exam. Chronic stress, on the other hand, presents an ongoing challenge that ultimately leads to feelings of being overwhelmed and may impair normal functioning, rendering us unable to attend school, for example. When the stress is acute, the individual usually adapts and all systems return to normal once the threat has passed. However, when the stress is chronic, the ongoing effects of the stress hormones on the body may be long lasting and increase the risk for immune system and inflammatory disease, jeopardizing overall health (McEwen and Gianaros 2010). The risk for heart attack increases as a result of the effects of stress on the cardiovascular system (McEwen and Stellar). Respiratory changes can trigger asthma attacks or panic attacks in some people. Headaches occur from constant tension of the muscles around the neck and shoulders. Maybe most alarming is the increased vulnerability to infection and inflammatory conditions such as arthritis, obesity, and certain cancers from the prolonged effects of stress on the immune system (Miller et. al. 2004; Cohen, Janicki-Deverts, and Miller 2007).

You may experience your stress physically, as is the case with a tension headache. You may also experience stress emotionally. Fatigue and/or difficulty concentrating are two ways that stress may be expressed emotionally. However, symptoms of stress may look very different in your child. She may feel "butterflies" in her stomach or complain of a stomachache. If she's feeling stressed she may want to sleep more or she may begin to have a hard time keeping up with her schoolwork. Any significant change in your child's behavior may be a sign that she's worried about something. It doesn't matter whether you think she has reason to be stressed or not. What matters is that she is feeling stressed. You may tell her that it's not important what other people think about her clothes, for example, but this doesn't change the reality that her stress response has been triggered; if she's feeling stressed, she may experience many of the physiological signs and symptoms of stress (refer to table 1 in chapter 1).

The longer the mind feels stressed, the longer these effects will continue to occur in the body. Knowing how the effects of chronic stress can lead to poor health, you may be wondering what can be done about it. Is it possible to reverse this process or turn the switch to off? The answer is yes. Let's look at the relaxation response, which deactivates the stress reaction.

The Relaxation Response

Famed Harvard physician and researcher Dr. Herbert Benson, of the Mind-Body Institute, first described the relaxation response in 1975. It is "an inducible physiologic state of quietude," the opposite of the stress reaction (Benson and

Klipper 1975/2000, xvii). This response turns off the switch that was activated by the "stressor." It helps to lower heart rate. Breathing rate slows and each breath becomes a little less shallow, a little deeper. Blood pressure is reduced and the muscles relax. In essence, you feel better, calmer.

Dr. Benson's team described four essential components that they believed were necessary to elicit the relaxation response: (1) a quiet environment; (2) a mental device (sound, word, phrase, or prayer repeated silently or aloud, or a fixed gaze on an object); (3) a passive attitude (not worrying about how well one is performing the technique and simply putting aside distracting thoughts to return to one's focus); and (4) a comfortable body position. Dr. Benson and his group later found that only two of these components were actually required to elicit this response: a mental device and a passive attitude (Benson and Klipper 1975/2000, xviii–xix).

How does mindfulness help to induce the relaxation response? The practices help the mind perceive that you are safe by focusing your attention in the present moment. Living in the present moment helps to shift the way in which you perceive the world. Noticing your breathing on a regular basis is one example of a practice that can promote this shift. When you turn your attention to your breathing without feeling the need to change anything, you are able to let go of your worries regarding the past and the future. You gently drift back to the present moment, where all is well.

It can be very helpful to practice noticing your breathing when you are feeling stressed. At a time when you find yourself worrying about something, try this simple exercise:

PARENT EXERCISE:
Follow Your Breath

1. Take a moment to just pay attention to your breathing. You don't need to change anything about it; just notice each inhalation and exhalation.

2. As you focus on your breath, look for the pause in your breathing pattern between each breath. This is the moment between the end of the out-breath and the beginning of the next in-breath. There is silence here.

3. Allow your mind to rest here in the silence. When you find the pause between each breath, say to yourself silently, "Rest."

4. Continue this practice for a count of ten breaths.

5. Now turn your attention to your body and see if you can identify any changes, such as softer shoulders, slower and deeper breathing, a relaxed belly, and so on.

You can keep a mental tally of what you noticed after completing the above exercise, or you may want to document these experiences in a journal or notebook. The key here is to increase your awareness of how you feel both when your attention is in the present moment and when it is not.

Practice the following breathing exercise with your child:

CHILD EXERCISE: Calming Breath

1. Tell your child to find a sitting position that is comfortable. Once she confirms that she is comfortable, tell her to simply notice her breathing.

2. Tell her, "You don't have to change anything just notice the air as it moves in through your nose and out through your mouth. With each breath in, think 'in.' With each breath out, think 'out'."

3. Some children may become distracted by thoughts that arise when they are doing this exercise. Let your child know that it is okay if she becomes distracted. You can suggest that she gently blow the thoughts away with each out-breath, like blowing the seeds off of a dandelion. She can then return her attention to her breathing.

4. Have her continue to notice her breathing for approximately three minutes. (If your child becomes very restless, you may start with one minute of practice and gradually lengthen the time that she sits until you reach three minutes.)

5. After the time has elapsed, tell her to open her eyes when she's ready.

6. Ask her what she felt during this exercise and give her an opportunity to share her experience with you. There is no right or wrong response here. I encourage you to share with her what you noticed as well.

If your child is ten to twelve years old, encourage her to practice this exercise once or twice daily on her own; if your child is younger than ten, she should practice once or twice a day with you. With regular practice, your child will soon have a tool that she can use to help reduce stress and promote relaxation.

When I have watched children practice the breath awareness exercises, I notice several things that are common to almost all of them. Their breathing slows and becomes more comfortable. Their shoulders soften and relax down and away from their ears. You can see them beginning to let the chair support their weight. Depending on the age of your child, she may not be able to describe all of the changes she experienced. But ask her if she feels better, worse, or about the same, and she will likely say, "I feel better," even when it's not clear to her why.

How do you know if the relaxation response has been triggered for your child? Look for the following signs:

- Slower breathing

- Deeper breaths

- Relaxed shoulders

- Softer belly

- Relaxed body posture

- Calm face

See how many other differences you can find. Once you have identified these, you and your child can add your own observations to this list.

If we know that the relaxation response can help children feel better when they are experiencing stress and that mindfulness induces the relaxation response, why aren't more children practicing mindfulness? Let's think about where we first learn how to manage stress.

Where Do We Learn to Manage Stress?

In our early elementary school years we learn how to read and write and do basic math. At home, we're taught good manners and the difference between right and wrong. But where do we learn how to handle our stress? In our society, we do not actively teach children how to cope with their worries and stresses in a healthy way. Stress management is a topic that's often not actively discussed in the home. Resiliency is not taught as part of the primary school curriculum. Because you probably did not receive any formal training in stress management when you were a child, you may be at a loss regarding how to help your own child. How do you teach something that you do not completely understand yourself? How do you model healthy coping strategies when you still struggle?

Children listen to what we say, but they more consistently watch what we do. Without knowing it, we model unhealthy coping strategies for our children on a regular basis. Our kids are learning from us, other adults, and their caretakers, in addition to older siblings and peers. They learn unhealthy coping strategies when we respond to their stress-fueled behavior with our own stress-fueled behavior. What parent cannot identify with the frustration that arises from dealing with a crying child in the grocery store or a kid throwing a tantrum on the floor in the middle of the mall? While the location and circumstances may change, we've all been there at some point in time. Through our frustration and embarrassment we may find it difficult to look deeper to understand what may fuel this behavior. You may end up responding to this inappropriate behavior by offering to give your child something she wants in order to quiet the behavior, or you may use fear by threatening to remove privileges in order to modify the behavior. Reinforcing negative behavior as a discipline strategy often results in frustration and a feeling of being out of control, since we know that the behavior is likely to reappear.

Discipline literally means "to teach"—so what should you teach your child in moments like this?

How Can Mindfulness Help?

Mindfulness is the practice of paying attention to your life in the present moment without judging what you notice. It is a way of exploring the inner life instead of focusing outwardly. This new way of noticing your world and yourself in the world will open your eyes to many insights. You will become aware of just how much your thoughts directly influence your emotions. We naturally act out how we are feeling, even when we don't understand why we're acting the way we are. Through mindfulness, you will learn to pay attention to your child's thoughts and emotions—not just her behaviors—when she is stressed, and you can help her learn how to assess her own thought process. Try the following exercise to practice building this skill with your child.

CHILD EXERCISE: Helping Your Child to Notice Thoughts

Find a quiet space in your home that is free of distractions (such as TV, telephones, and other family members) to practice this exercise with your child.

1. Tell your child that you are going to play a game together. The object of the game is to find the thoughts that hide inside our minds.

2. Have her sit comfortably in a chair or on the floor.

3. Invite your child to close her eyes. Tell her that for this exercise she's going to use her inner eyes to look around inside of her mind.

4. Say "We're going to take a trip to the beach. Use your imagination to see yourself sitting on the sand watching the waves roll onto the shore and back out into the ocean." The waves can follow the pattern of her breathing, rolling in with each in-breath and back out with each out-breath. Count five breaths as she watches the waves.

5. Tell her to remember a time when she was feeling sad. Give her a few moments to remember.

6. Encourage her to pay attention to the thought(s) inside her mind that made her feel sad. Once she sees the thought, she can place it on the sand. The waves will come ashore and wash the thought away into the ocean.

7. Have her repeat this process with each thought that she sees until there are no more thoughts coming up for this sad experience.

8. She can now pay attention to her breathing for five breaths to help her return to the present moment before she opens her eyes.

9. Ask her what made her sad. What was her behavior like when she felt sad? How did she act? What was the outcome? Did her actions help her to feel better, or did she feel worse?

10. Ask her to tell you the thoughts that she noticed when she was feeling sad. Help her to see the connection between what she was thinking (the thoughts), how she was feeling (the emotion, in this case sadness), and how she reacted (her behavior). Point out the fact that this exercise gives her a way to wash away some of the thoughts that are making her feel bad.

The beach has always been a calming place for me and my son. If you like, replace the beach scene with other places (and metaphors) that bring peace and calm to you and your family. Also, feel free to use this exercise to examine other emotions in addition to sadness and identify the thoughts that relate to the emotion. Use recent situations in which you and your child were unhappy with the consequences of her behavior.

Helping your child to become aware of the initial thoughts that are driving her behavior is a key first step in helping her to modify her behavior. The above exercise is a nonthreatening way to help her explore these connections and develop strategies to defuse her stress and respond to these situations in a healthy way. Committing to a daily mindfulness practice for yourself and your child will provide nurturing and support as you face life's joys and challenges on this journey.

Living in the Present Moment

In our fast-paced world we seldom find time to just "be." We fill our lives with activities, write long to-do lists—we're in motion from sunup to sundown. So many things need to get done, and we systematically go through the day checking items off along the way. Kids fed, dressed, and dropped off at school—check. Work e-mail opened and read—check. Meetings attended and reports written—check. Groceries picked up, dinner prepared—check. On and on this goes, day after day, keeping us from truly experiencing the moments that make up our lives. Have you ever arrived at home from your evening commute and had no recollection of actually driving home? Or perhaps you've been sitting with your child as she shares her day with you only to find that you didn't really hear a word that she said. With so much to do, adults and kids barely notice the routine activities of our day, much less our emotional state.

In between activities, our thoughts sometimes take over, ranging from regrets about the past to worries about what the future holds. When was the last time you remember being in the moment? You may find that this is true for your child as well. She may worry about how life will change in the future, or she may be sad about events that have occurred in the past.

But when we enter the present, it may seem as if time stands still. When you are fully present in life, you do not feel stressed; rather, you feel energized.

INCREASING AWARENESS OF OUR DAILY HABITS

Kids and many adults are disconnected from activities that occur every single day. We take thousands of steps throughout our day without actually noticing how we get from point A to point B, without appreciating the ordinary sights and sounds that fill our day. Our kids sit through classes for the majority of the day, often unaware of the multitude of thoughts that scroll through the mind, like news headlines that scroll across the bottom of your TV screen.

It's important for us to notice the daily activities, rituals, and processes that we take for granted. There is information waiting for us when we notice the smaller details of our life—it is to be found in our thoughts, in our breath, and in our bodies. Noticing how you think, feel, and act as you perform these daily rituals can provide great insight into what lifts you up and what brings you down. Your heightened attention to these areas of your life will make it easier to be more alert to what is happening within the present moment; as a result, you will experience life more completely.

With mindful practices, you increase your awareness of these simple yet powerful processes that will sustain you throughout your life. The following are examples of a few life activities that often go unnoticed among both parents and children.

Breathing

Of all the things we take for granted, this is likely the biggest. You breathe eighteen to twenty-four times per minute, every hour of every day, year after year. And we can gain a lot of information by paying attention to our breathing patterns. For example, it is not uncommon for us to hold our breath when we get nervous or anxious, and breathing may become shallow and rapid when we're scared or upset. Helping your child learn to focus on the breath can provide her with insight into her emotional state.

Walking

In the morning, we get out of bed and walk to the bathroom to groom ourselves for the day. We walk to the car or school bus, from class to class, or throughout the office all day long, without giving much thought to our physical body and all that it does to support us. We're also unaware of the multiple environments that we move in and out of throughout the day.

Many people think of meditation as sitting cross-legged on a mountaintop, chanting a phrase repeatedly. Although this may be a part of some meditation practices, mindfulness incorporates both sitting and movement practices, such as walking. Walking can provide many benefits to you and your child to promote stress reduction, including the production of endorphins, also known as "natural pain relievers." More important, mindful walking allows you to move through your environment while maintaining present-moment awareness. Have you ever noticed that the sky is not a uniform shade of blue, or that clouds move at different speeds and some don't seem to move at all? An activity such as walking can become a new experience when you use your five senses to appreciate the world around you.

Eating

Food represents a variety of things to people. At a basic level, it is the fuel that our bodies need in order to stay healthy and indeed alive. It is also used in celebrations and to comfort us when we're feeling ill or sad. But in our busy, overscheduled lives, food is increasingly being used without awareness and in the absence of hunger. We find ourselves eating on the go, in the car while commuting, at our desks while multitasking, and mindlessly in front of the television. Have you ever finished a meal and not been able to remember what you just ate? Our kids are learning to do this too.

Mindfulness can help your child sense the difference among feelings of hunger, satiety, and fullness. She will begin to notice if she is eating at a time when she is not hungry, and she will learn to explore what she may really be hungry for (such as companionship). Paying attention to what we eat can lead to a more enjoyable experience of our meals and help us establish a healthier relationship with food.

Sleeping

Sleep is something we all need in adequate quantities, but few of us get optimal amounts. Sleep aids are increasingly being prescribed in the United States. We're seeing more and more sleep disturbances in our children as well. Kids report to me that they find it hard to "turn off" at night and go to sleep. Others say that they fall asleep quickly because they're so exhausted, only to awaken during the night.

These problems may be due in part to the environment in which we try to rest. Children go to bed with the television on. Others are playing video games or logged on to the computer right up until the moment of bedtime. The quality and quantity of sleep may suffer when kids are constantly overstimulated in this way. As a result of outside stimulation, they miss important cues that are designed to tell them when they need rest. Using mindfulness can help kids acknowledge the thoughts floating around in their head and help them learn the skills needed in order to release these thoughts in a healthy way, which can help to calm the mind and invite peaceful and restorative rest.

Thinking

Thoughts come and go in our minds constantly. You're having thoughts now as you're reading this book. Thoughts are neutral; they cannot harm us unless we let them. It's the meaning that we assign to our thoughts that brings us either joy or pain. The problem is that we are usually unaware of the thoughts that we are having. Setting aside time to pay attention to our thoughts can provide us with tremendous insight into our emotional state and help us better understand our actions.

Using the mindfulness practices found in part 2 of this book, you will learn how to start applying mindfulness during your daily mindless routines and activities, such as breathing, eating, and walking, and teach them to your child. Intermediate and advanced skills such as loving-kindness and visualization will also be taught. These simple, practical strategies will reduce the risk of stress-related conditions that negatively affect health.

When you frequently take time to center yourself, you will find it much easier to get back on track when life's challenges blow you off course. The more you practice, the more you will begin to use these skills in real-world situations to help yourself and your child to navigate the sometimes-turbulent waters of life.

HEALTHY COPING: HELPING YOUR CHILD BUILD A TOOLKIT

The exercises taught in this book provide various examples of specific mindful practices. This variety is necessary, because each child may have a natural affinity for one or two practices over the others. If your child has a lot of energy and needs to move often, for example, she may enjoy the movement practices more than the sitting exercises. All of the exercises are designed to foster nonjudgmental awareness and a greater sense of well-being. The main objective is to build the skills by practicing on a daily basis. If your child plays a musical instrument or plays a team sport, she will understand the need for regular practice. The idea is that she will develop these skills for use on a daily basis in addition to feeling more prepared when a major life event occurs. Remind your child to use her tools when she is feeling stressed or anxious and that she can carry the tools with her wherever she goes.

Incorporating Mindful Practices into Daily Living

The challenge of learning this new information is to figure out how to incorporate it into a busy life. I'd encourage you to start by selecting one of the ten mindful practices (listed in the introduction) to focus on. Set aside a defined period of time for practicing the principles each day. You may start with five or ten minutes per day and gradually increase this time as you become more comfortable with the practices. The important thing is to practice. Ultimately, the goal is to practice regularly enough that you find you are living a mindful life.

The following section of this book explores each of the ten mindful practices presented in the introduction. Read through each chapter and use the stories and exercises to familiarize yourself and your child with these concepts. The mindful practices do not need to be done in order. Begin with the one that you feel is most applicable for you and your child in that moment. Over time, with regular practice, you will find that you seamlessly blend these concepts into all aspects of your life. As you continue to teach your child and model healthy stress management, your child will also incorporate these concepts into her life.

Are you ready? Let the journey begin!

PART II

3

Awareness of Breathing

Breathe. Let go. And remind yourself that this very
moment is the only one you know you have for sure.

—Oprah Winfrey

I continue to be awestruck when I have the opportunity to witness a baby's first breath. The breath represents the vital energy that is synonymous with life. Allowing the breath to flow naturally in and out of our lungs brings a sense of calm and peacefulness, a feeling that everything is in order. Increasing your awareness of the breath is one simple yet powerful way to anchor yourself in the moment.

LIVING IN THE PRESENT MOMENT

"Time flies when you're having fun." It's a saying that you've heard many times before, but what does it really mean? Why does time pass so quickly when you're having fun? If you think back to times in your life when time seemed to fly, you're likely to find that you were engrossed in a particular activity or event, immersed in what you were experiencing. Some people say that when they are in this state of mind, time seems to simultaneously fast-forward and pause—to both fly and stand still at the same time. Our experience of the passage of time when we are living in the present is different from how we perceive it when we are thinking about the past or future. When you are able to stay in the moment, life is richer. In the present moment, your awareness is heightened and attention is increased.

LEARNING TO RETURN TO CENTER

When life becomes unmanageable, you may feel that you have no control over your circumstances, emotions, or behavior.

3/20/2019

HEINZER KATHRIN

All Contra Costa County Libraries will be
closed on Sunday, April 21st. Items may
be renewed at ccclib.org or by calling
1-800-984-4636, menu option 1. Book drops
will be open. El Sobrante Library remains
closed for repairs.

Hold Shelf Slip

Your child probably feels the same way. What can you do when you're feeling powerless? You can return to the present moment. When you feel pushed into the future or pulled into the past by your thinking, remind yourself to gently return to center.

Think of an anchor. It allows a sailing vessel to remain in place and not drift off. Your breath is your anchor. When you turn your attention to your breathing, you are brought back to the present moment. How do you do this? Simply focus on each breath. There is no need to change your breathing; you're just paying attention to it. This automatically triggers the relaxation response. You're likely to notice that your breathing rate slows down. You may also become aware of tension leaving your body. This simple shift in your thinking can help calm the waters when you're in the midst of a storm.

■ John's Story

Today is John's birthday. "Ten. I'm in the double digits now," John thinks. He rolls over onto his back, looking up at the early morning sky through his bedroom window. He thinks to himself about what it means to be a "tween" (the stage between middle childhood and adolescence). Next year he'll finish elementary school and then start middle school. "Middle school," he thinks. "It must be so much harder than elementary school. The kids are a lot bigger, too. What if I don't fit in? I'll have to change classes, too. What if I can't keep up with my schoolwork and my grades fall?" All of these thoughts and questions swirl around in John's mind like debris caught in a whirlwind. It all feels so intense to John.

What just happened with John? He had a "thought attack." A thought attack occurs when we make up a story about the past or the future and allow our thoughts around that story to spin out of control. It's usually triggered by a single initiating thought. John propelled himself into the future, and all of a sudden he was seeing himself as a middle school misfit with failing grades. These worries were triggered by his initial thought, "What does it mean to be a 'tween'?" This happened to John often. When asked how he feels during these thought attacks, he said he feels like he's drowning; it's as if he can't catch his breath.

When questioned further, John realized that he was actually holding his breath at times like this. So John was taught to pay attention to his breath when these thoughts started to build. He didn't need to do anything else. Like most boys, he was pretty skeptical that something so simple would help, but he was willing to give it a try. What he noticed was that his breathing automatically slowed down when he paid attention to it. He also found that he was taking deeper breaths. He felt better.

This simple step, paying attention to your breathing, can work wonders for your child. When John was asked to simply notice his breathing, it accomplished two things: (1) it allowed him to focus on something other than the thoughts that were triggering his emotional distress, and (2) it triggered the relaxation response, which helped him to feel calmer in a matter of moments. This tool can provide your child with a sense of control when he's feeling out of control. With practice, your child will be able to add this to his toolkit, to use whenever and wherever he may need it.

MINDFUL PRACTICE EXERCISE:
Finding Your Anchor

Practicing new mindfulness skills with your child is a great way to reinforce them in your child's mind and incorporate them into your own life, allowing you to parent mindfully.

1. Tell your child to find a comfortable sitting position on a chair, a mat, or the floor.

2. Invite him to close his eyes gently and take a deep breath.

3. Instruct him to just pay attention to his breathing. You can say, "Notice your breathing as the air moves in and out of your nose or mouth." Have him "watch" the breath and follow it as it moves in and out for a few breaths.

4. Have him find the pause in his breathing pattern—at the end of the inhaling breath but before the start of the exhaling breath. The pause is a brief moment, but it exists in each breath. Ask your child to look for this point. This is a place where he can rest his attention. Many children who are task oriented will be fully immersed in the activity of finding the pause. This helps to keep your child anchored in the present moment.

5. Have your child continue to find the pause within the breath until he's completed ten breaths (one breath equals one inhalation and one exhalation).

6. Once he has completed the exercise, ask him to open his eyes whenever he's ready. Help him explore what this activity was like for him. Ask him, "What was that like for you? What did you notice about your breathing?" Debriefing in this way allows for self-reflection that may lead to an increased connection between his mind and body. With regular practice, this process aids in your child's personal growth and maturation.

You may want to count the repetitions out loud for your child so that he can focus on the breath. As he becomes more skilled or if he's practicing alone, he can use his fingers to count out the ten breaths. Engaging in this practice once or twice daily can help your child trigger the relaxation response, bringing instant calm in most situations. Remind your child that he can practice this exercise whenever he is feeling worried or stressed out about something. A phrase such as "Remember your breath" can help trigger your child to use this tool in the midst of a distressing situation.

This exercise is also a valuable practice for you as a parent. When your child is anxious and worried, it may fuel your own stress. The rapid escalation of your stress may lead to a variety of uncomfortable emotions in you, including surprise, fear, sadness, and anger. Rather than choosing to sit with these uncomfortable feelings and be present to what we are experiencing in the moment, we may get lost in our thoughts about the situation and react rather than respond. Using the breath to anchor you in the present moment gives you time to trigger the relaxation response, allowing a sense of calm to develop. In this calmer state, you can then choose how you would like to respond to the current situation.

The anchored breath can provide a sense of security for both you and your child. It is a safety net where you can rest in the midst of an emotional storm, knowing that the calm will return and that you will be okay when the storm is over. I am confident that this will become one of the frequently used items in your (and your child's) toolkit.

4

Relaxation Breathing

Give your stress wings and let it fly away.

—Terri Guillemets

One of the highlights of first grade for me was "rest time." Ms. Becker would announce that it was time to get out our mats and lie down. Although most of us kids were not sleepy and had stopped taking naps a year or two earlier, it was an opportunity to allow our mind and body to recharge and prepare for the activities of the afternoon. Ms. Becker was so wise. In our fast-paced society, we do not place enough emphasis on the value of rest and relaxation. The information in this chapter will provide tools for you to get your child started successfully balancing relaxation with the busyness of life.

INITIATING THE RELAXATION RESPONSE

Spring is one of my favorite times of year. Everything is new and fresh. Bulbs that were planted in the fall are pushing up through the ground. The birds are happily singing in the warming air. The days are longer and brighter compared to those of the winter season. For many, spring represents renewal, but we often overlook the importance of the rest that winter provided.

Kids are as busy as adults these days. On most days they spend six hours or more in school, consumed with class assignments and positive and negative social interactions with peers. Add extracurricular activities, homework, chores, and an evening meal and you begin to see how little time may be leftover for creative play or relaxation.

Dr. Herbert Benson, renowned Harvard professor and founder of the Mind-Body Medicine Institute in Massachusetts, describes the relaxation response as "a physical state of deep rest that changes the physical and emotional responses to stress"

(Benson-Henry Institute for Mind-Body Medicine n.d.). It is the opposite of the fight-or-flight response. This state of deep rest is extremely important, as it allows the body and mind to reconnect, bringing the attention back to the present moment. In nature, many plants go dormant during the winter. Their leaves are lost, but root systems continue to grow and prepare for the blossoming that will come in spring. Rest and relaxation permits time for quiet contemplation. It is from this place that your child can see more clearly, allowing her to return to a state of calm, where she can make more informed decisions.

AN OPPORTUNITY TO REST

We spend much of our energy on *doing* and seldom leave time to just *be*. In fact, we're so accustomed to doing something all the time that we may forget how to rest. Resting is a natural state for young children. As a child gets older she may tend to forget how to let go of the busyness and just relax. You and your child may need help in remembering how to rest.

Why is rest important? Relaxation is the first step in releasing negative tension and worries. Releasing stress (via the relaxation response) allows for pure rest. This deep rest is important because it frees up the energy of the mind and body to focus on restorative functions.

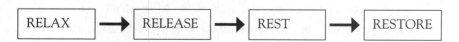

RELAX → RELEASE → REST → RESTORE

When practiced regularly, this restoration results in an enhanced immune system, improved ability to concentrate, and increased feelings of calm and well-being. Some parents ask, "Doesn't this happen during sleep?" For some children, it does. Unfortunately, for many children this is not the case. The majority of kids get less than the recommended ten to eleven hours of sleep per night. To make matters worse, the quality of sleep is frequently inadequate due to lack of a bedtime routine, poor sleep habits, night awakening, and other distractions (such as TV). To see how relaxation breathing can make a difference in the life of your child, take a look at Sarah's story.

■ Sarah's Story

Sarah is in kindergarten. She loves school. She gets to play with her friends, and Miss Williams makes learning so much fun. Everything was great until Sarah's mother went into the hospital. Sarah had never spent any time away from her mother before. After three days her mother came home but Sarah was still worried. What would happen if her mother needed to go back to the hospital? What if she didn't come back home that time?

Sarah had a hard time letting go of these upsetting thoughts, and she was afraid to let her mother out of her sight. Her mother would put her to bed but she couldn't fall asleep. She began to climb into her parents' bed each night so she could be near her mother. She was able to fall asleep there; she felt that her mother was safe if she was nearby.

This situation was difficult for Sarah's parents. They tried to put her back to bed each night, to no avail. As the nights wore on, it seemed simpler to just let Sarah stay in their bed so everyone could get some sleep. When her parents brought Sarah to my office, I asked her why she wasn't sleeping at night. Sarah replied that she needed to stay awake in case her mother needed her. This was a surprise to her mother. After some discussion, we determined that

Sarah was too worried and stressed to fall asleep easily and stay asleep; she was restless. We talked to Sarah about the fact that sometimes people get sick and have to go to the hospital, and that this wasn't Sarah's fault—she couldn't have prevented it.

We decided to try relaxation breathing as a strategy to help Sarah let go of some of her worrisome thoughts. Her mother would also use this breathing practice to help her reduce her own stress and support her mental and emotional health. So Sarah's mother helped her to practice each night after her bath as a part of her bedtime ritual. Sarah was told that with each deep breath the negative thoughts and worries were being released. She didn't have to hold on to them anymore. After ten days, Sarah's mother called to say that Sarah had slept through the night for the first time since the hospital stay, and in her own bed! She was delighted and Sarah felt good about herself.

Relaxation breathing provided a way for Sarah to trigger the relaxation response. Once this occurred, Sarah was able to release the negative thoughts she was holding about her mother's health. Releasing these worries allowed her to rest, giving her the time her mind and body needed to restore her normal sleep pattern. Sarah was also told that if her mother did need to go back to the hospital, the relaxation breathing could help her to deal with how she was feeling.

Teach this technique to your child and apply it to stressful situations that your child may be facing. With regular practice, you and your child will build the skills to successfully interrupt the stress response and produce feelings of calm instead.

When kids are stressed or anxious, it is not unusual for them to hold their breath or take shallow breaths, often without being aware of it. These shallow breaths cause the breathing rate to increase and can lead to several changes within the body that may cause further stress and anxiety. Taking deep breaths can help your child slow her breathing and allow her mind and body to relax. Try the exercise below with your child before bedtime or in the midst of a stressful day.

MINDFUL PRACTICE EXERCISE:
Calming Belly Breaths

1. Invite your child to sit in a relaxed position. She may sit on a chair or on a comfortable mat on the floor.

2. Direct her to turn her attention to her breathing. Tell her to notice the air as it moves into her lungs when she breathes in through her nose, and to follow the air as she breathes out through her mouth. Have her take approximately four breaths in this way.

3. Next, instruct her to place the palm of one hand on her belly. Her palm should be centered over her navel. Tell her to feel her hand move outward with her belly as she takes a deep breath in. Have her picture the air moving in through her nose and traveling all the way down into her belly; tell her to notice her belly as it blows up like a balloon. As she exhales, all of the air flows out of her belly and up through her nose; she should notice that with each exhalation her belly flattens and her hand moves inward, toward her center. With each inhale she invites the breath (not forcing it) into her belly, and

with each exhale she gently releases the breath as the air flows out, letting the belly go soft. Repeat this process for about ten breaths.

4. Remind her that when she is faced with a stressful situation, she can use this technique to help her calm down and feel more relaxed. She can begin to ask herself, "Am I holding stress or worry?" If the answer is yes, she can practice her belly breathing.

5. Ask her to check in with her body to see how she is feeling (relaxed, calm, happy, sad). Ask her to notice her breathing—is it fast or is it slow and relaxed? It's okay if she doesn't feel relaxed in the beginning. Some children may work really hard, expecting a certain outcome. This fuels the stress response. Remind her that she's just noticing what is happening.

6. Try variations of this exercise by adding phrases to repeat while watching the belly. For example, when the belly expands on the inhale she might say "Calm" and, on the exhale, "Mind." With the next breath say "Calm" and "Body." Alternate these phrases with each breathing set. Ask your child to think of other phrases to try. Making this exercise fun will increase the likelihood that your child will want to practice more often.

Spending time relaxing and allowing ourselves to experience being rather than doing is an effective way to minimize the impact of chronic stress. Make time for you and your child to relax each day, individually and together. Starting with just five minutes a day will help you develop a new habit. Prioritizing this time for your child is important. Remember that you serve as a role model for your child, so ensure that you are taking time for yourself as well. Developing these healthy life skills to cope with daily stress will build your child's resiliency as she learns to replace anxiety with feelings of calm.

5

Mindful Walking

To find new things, take the path you took yesterday.

—John Burroughs

Research has shown that being outside in nature makes people feel more alive (Ryan et al. 2010). Children are meant to move; it's one way that a child learns to explore the natural world. Combining walking and other forms of movement with time spent in nature can help your child to appreciate his surroundings and develop a rich moment-to-moment awareness of life's experiences.

CONNECTING WITH THE ENVIRONMENT

In the summer of 2009, I was fortunate enough to spend some time in Hawaii. The island of Kauai is one of the most beautiful places I've ever visited. You can see the horizon from almost any spot on the island. The stars seem brighter than they do on the mainland and the air is clear. One day as I was sitting on the balcony to my room I noticed a small spider. She seemed very busy gliding gracefully from one corner of a railing to another. I watched in amazement as this small creature deliberately and persistently wove an intricate web. She was challenged by strong tropical breezes that blew her back and forth but she continued on, seemingly unfazed. I was completely absorbed in watching this activity, fully present in the moment as I looked on with curiosity. I've seen many spiderwebs before but I'd never been witness to the creation of one. It's such a simple thing, yet so complex. So often, we move through our environment, often walking blindly past the many wonders along the path. When we stop to observe what is taking place all around us, we are struck by how fascinating nature is. Connecting with nature transports us from our thoughts of the past and our worries about the future to the here and now. Exploring your environment with your child is a fantastic way to practice mindfulness.

FINDING SOMETHING NEW IN THE FAMILIAR

You don't need to travel to Hawaii or wait for a vacation to connect with the environment. Take advantage of all that your community has to offer. Instead of rushing along the same path you take to work and/or school each day, pay attention to what is around you. There is so much to notice—the different leaves on the neighborhood trees, the brilliant colors of the plants, the movement of the earthworm over a cement sidewalk after the rain, the outline of buildings against the blue sky, and the multiple sounds of traffic as cars are driving by. A new and exciting world is available to you and your child as you both learn to pay attention to the things you normally fail to notice on your journey.

■ Sean's Story

Sean was struggling in school. He had done well in kindergarten through second grade, but third grade was so much harder. He found it very hard to concentrate on what the teacher was saying. He studied every day, but when he was called on in class the information wasn't there in his head anymore. This made school very stressful for him and not as enjoyable as it once had been.

Sean's parents took him to see a psychologist to have an evaluation, and they learned that Sean had attention deficit/ hyperactivity disorder (ADHD). Sean wasn't happy to hear this news. He knew of other kids who had ADHD—they had to go to the office to take medicine, and the other kids made fun of them. Sean's parents wanted to know what else they could do to help Sean succeed in class in addition to the medication prescribed. In addition to his difficulty retaining information, Sean seemed to have trouble sitting still in class. He knew he needed to stay in his seat, but it was so hard. He felt a lot of pressure to "be good."

We brainstormed several options, including ensuring that he was getting proper rest and nutrition, and mindful walking—which I have noticed has been quite helpful to many children with ADHD. Sean loved the outdoors, so we decided to have him take a nature walk each day after school, so he could practice being mindful. We encouraged him to look for something new every day. He started with a walk in the backyard. Walking around, he noticed birds that he hadn't seen before. His father guided him to notice the variety of colors on the birds, the different sizes of leaves on the trees, and even the bugs crawling on the trunk of one tree! Over time, Sean's parents found that this activity helped Sean to relieve some of the excess energy that he had stored up from sitting in school all day. What was even more surprising was the improved concentration that Sean now had. He was able to use his mindfulness practice to focus and pay attention in a more meaningful way in the classroom. He also used mindfulness to help alleviate some of the negative feelings that surfaced in class when he was stressed.

Walking is a simple way to teach mindfulness to your child. Try the exercise below and discover the benefits of mindful walking.

MINDFUL PRACTICE EXERCISE:
Take a Walk on a Treasure Hunt

1. Tell your child that you're going to go on a treasure hunt together. If he doesn't know what a treasure hunt is, take a moment to explain it to him.

2. Tell him that you will look for all the "treasures" in your environment—things that we may not usually notice because they're there all the time. Explain that you will appreciate and give thanks for these "treasures" by noticing them on your walk.

3. Give him information about where the walk will take place—indoors or outdoors, on the street where you live, in the park, or inside your home, for example. Give him the following guidelines for your walk:

4. "You may walk slowly or quickly or somewhere in between—whatever feels most comfortable to you. You may pass others while you are walking. You may walk forward, backward, or sideways. Make it fun!

5. "Use your senses and pay attention to what you see and hear; pay attention to the things that you can touch. Breathe in the air and see if you notice any new or familiar smells/odors. As you walk, pay attention to how your body feels as it moves. What are the movements that your body must go through in order for you to walk? What do you feel under the bottom of your feet when you take your steps?"

6. Once you've reviewed the guidelines, ask him if he has any questions. Once his questions are answered, begin the walk. Plan to spend approximately eight to ten minutes on this walk.

7. After a few minutes of the walking meditation, have him walk really fast and then run really fast for a few seconds. Prompt him to notice his environment by pointing out sights and sounds that you see and hear. Then take a break to rest. Ask him to share the treasures he has found so far.

8. Have him walk as slowly as he can possibly can for a few seconds.

9. Ask him to come to a complete stop and just stand still for a few moments.

10. Prompt him to decide at what speed he would like to walk home.

11. When you return home, tell him to take a few deep breaths. Spend some time hearing what "treasures" he found on the walk. Find out what he enjoyed most about walking this way. Have him check in with his body to see how he's feeling (relaxed, calm, happy, or sad, for example). Remind him that he can use this exercise as a tool to help him when he's feeling worried, stressed, or sad.

Mindful walking is a fun way to teach kids to practice the art of paying attention. Practice the above exercise at least once daily. Even if you don't have a lot of time, you can decide to be mindful for the first ten steps of your day or when taking ten steps to move from one activity to the next. You can also include a longer walk as part of your child's sixty minutes of daily physical activity (the amount of exercise recommended for kids).

Find creative ways to add mindful walking to your child's daily routine. Turn a simple after-dinner walk into a mindful exercise by using all your senses to explore your surroundings. Pay attention to sights, sounds, textures, and odors. Look for things you haven't noticed before. Feel the sensations within your own body as you take each step and move through the environment. Share what you are feeling and seeing with your child.

Encourage your child to use this technique on the playground and at school. The practice of mindful walking can bring a whole new world of awareness to children. It's also a great way for you to spend time with your child, get your body moving, and wind down after a long day.

6

Mindful Movement
with Yoga

Yoga teaches us to cure what need not be
endured and endure what cannot be cured.

—B. K. S. Iyengar

There are numerous yoga programs available to children today. Schools and community programs are offering classes to kids. DVDs, books, and online videos are just a few of the many resources that provide information on how to teach children about yoga. Teachers, parents, and kids all report many benefits for participating in such activities. The true value of having your child learn and practice the principles of yoga (asanas [poses], breathing, relaxation, diet, and meditation) is that it provides her with a holistic view of health that encompasses the mind, body, and spirit and a deeper understanding of her own self-worth.

DISCOVER YOUR BODY'S STRENGTH

As a pediatrician, I am the recipient of "gifts" from the children to whom I provide care. The gifts I'm referring to are the new accomplishments that my patients have achieved since the last visit. Young kids are eager to show off all the new skills that they have attained, in addition to changes they have noticed in their body. "Dr. Bailey, look what I can do!" After this exclamation boys and girls alike will often enthusiastically raise both arms and bend at the elbow, proudly displaying their biceps muscles, and bringing a smile to the faces of children, parents, and staff, myself included.

We often think of strength as solely a physical trait, such as a bulging muscle, but it is so much more. *Merriam-Webster's Collegiate Dictionary* defines *strength* as the "capacity for exertion or endurance…power to resist force…toughness" (Merriam-Webster Collegiate Dictionary, 11th ed., s.v. "strength").

In our culture, we demand much from our bodies without paying much attention to what *they* need: nurturing, love, and rest. Like adults, kids take for granted how hard the body works, with little appreciation for its capacity for rapid growth and development. Instead, many focus on what is wrong with the body. In the work that I do, I see many children who point out body flaws and imperfections. They wish they were taller, shorter, thinner, less hairy, more muscular, and on and on. If your child doesn't like what she sees when she looks in the mirror, she may begin to disconnect from her body by not paying much attention to it at all. As a result, your child may not be as connected with her body as she was when she was younger.

Hatha yoga can help your child reconnect with her body. Hatha yoga is a slow-paced, gentle form of yoga combining stretches with simple breathing exercises. This ancient yoga practice allows the body to connect with the mind through focused attention on the breath while simultaneously holding the pose. Awareness follows, letting your child see what the body can do when she releases her resistance and she relaxes into the pose. The aim of this practice is not to achieve a perfect pose; it's to notice subtle shifts within the body as your child achieves balance between her mind, body, and spirit.

DEVELOP A STRONG INNER CORE

Building a strong inner core (back and abdomen) leads to an overall increase in strength, coordination, and flexibility. It also provides a sturdy framework to support the body as it carries out its daily tasks and to support the mind in coping with daily stresses. Yoga is a fun way for kids to work on strengthening the inner core muscles. Through the use of imagination, your child will learn yoga poses while pretending to be an animal or object in nature.

■ Linda's Story

Linda was a beautiful twelve-year-old-girl who was unhappy with her weight. According to her mother, she looked like the women on her father's side of the family. Linda remembered a time when she was able to participate in sports and dance activities. When she came to my office, she had become ashamed of her body and felt betrayed by the multiple aches and pains that she experienced due to her excess weight. Linda was afraid that her body wouldn't cooperate with her if she signed up for dance classes or gymnastics. "My body just won't do what I ask it to do," she said. She was also worried about what other people thought about the way she looked; she'd been teased by both boys and girls on the school bus about her weight.

I knew that Linda really enjoyed art. She wanted to become an interior designer when she grew up. I asked her if she had ever heard of yoga, and she replied that she thought that yoga was painful and was pretty sure that she wouldn't be able to get her body into the positions she'd seen people doing on TV. We discussed yoga as a way for her to get in touch with her body and explore what it was capable of. Yoga, I said, might allow her to listen to the messages that her body was trying to give her.

She agreed to find a yoga DVD and practice at least three times per week. I invited her to keep a journal of the things she noticed after each yoga session. When she returned to the clinic four weeks later, she seemed very excited. She'd found a yoga DVD that she liked and had practiced three to four days per week since the last office visit. She was surprised and excited to discover how much her body could do. "Practicing yoga was like turning my body into art. It was so much fun!" She felt proud of her body for the first time in years. Her mother noted that Linda seemed more patient with her siblings and was not as hard on herself. She was calmer, too.

There are many benefits to yoga, including improvements in physical strength, balance, and flexibility. Introduce the following yoga exercises to your child as a way for her to explore all the wonderful things her body is capable of.

MINDFUL PRACTICE EXERCISE: Finding Your Strength Through Yoga

I recommend that your child wear loose and comfortable clothing for this exercise. Yoga is typically practiced with bare feet, so choose a surface that will not cause your child to slip and fall. You can lay a yoga mat or towel on the floor to make the floor exercises more comfortable. It's helpful to have a light blanket available to cover your child's body during the rest time. Remember to make it fun.

There are four parts to this exercise: deep breathing, gorilla warm-up, safari poses, and rest.

Invite your child to play a game where she gets to use her imagination. Tell her she's going to go on a safari. Tell her that she will pretend to be the different animals and landmarks that you find on your safari.

Deep Breathing

First, have her sit on the floor with her legs crossed and notice her breathing for four or five breaths. (Kids are encouraged to take deep breaths during yoga practice.)

Gorilla Warm-Up

Next, help your child warm up by pretending that she's a gorilla. From a standing position she should bend over and reach toward the floor. She can let gravity pull her body downward. Make sure she keeps her knees soft. She can sway from left to right in this position. Spend two to three minutes in this position.

Safari Poses

Have your child hold each pose below—Mountain, Lion, and Cobra—for thirty seconds for younger children (ages five to eight years) and two to three minutes for older children (ages nine to twelve years).

MOUNTAIN POSE

1. Have your child stand up tall with her feet shoulder-width apart and her arms down at her sides. She should feel her feet firmly connected to the floor. If she feels wobbly, ask her to focus on an object in front of her.

2. Ask her to notice her breathing and how her body feels as she stands tall and strong like the mountain.

LION (CAT) POSE

1. Now she can get down on the floor on all fours (hands and knees) while keeping the back straight.

2. She should take a deep breath in and arch her back like a cat does.

3. Have her straighten her back again during the breath out. She can roar like a lion as she is letting the air out of her lungs.

4. Repeat the two previous steps (breathing in and out) three times.

COBRA POSE

1. Have your child lie face down on the floor with her hands next to her chest.

2. While taking a deep breath in, she can slowly lift her chest until her arms are straight.

3. Have her hold this pose while taking slow, deep breaths in and out.

4. Return to the starting position; repeat once.

Rest Time

1. Have your child lie flat on her back with her legs straight.

2. Let her hands rest gently at her sides with the palms facing up.

3. While she takes slow, deep breaths, tell her to feel her body connected to the floor.

4. Let go of any tension with each out-breath, allowing the body to relax.

5. Rest in this pose for five to seven minutes.

Practice this exercise two to three times per week. You can incorporate this exercise as a part of your child's recommended sixty minutes of daily physical activity.

Yoga practiced mindfully can help your child foster a true appreciation for her body, increasing the likelihood that she'll be motivated to establish healthy habits to take better care of it. In addition, when practiced regularly, yoga is a wonderful way to cultivate self-compassion. For more information on helping your child develop a yoga practice, please see the resources section at the end of the book.

7

Mindful Eating

If we could give every individual the right amount of
nourishment and exercise, not too little and not too
much, we would have found the safest way to health.

—Hippocrates

Sharing food with family and friends is such a wonderful part of our culture. The community and connection that results as the food is prepared and savored together unites people from different backgrounds. With the hustle and bustle of our lives it is easy to miss out on opportunities to experience this connection not only with others but also with ourselves. Paying attention to the act of eating can provide more than just nourishment of the physical body.

THE JOY OF EATING

In 2005, I had the honor of attending a professional development workshop led by Dr. Rachel Naomi Remen at the Institute for the Study of Health and Illness at Commonweal. The retreat center was a coastal paradise located in beautiful Bolinas, California. I was looking forward to spending some time in this serene space. As I read through the program brochure I noticed that vegetarian meals would be provided during the length of the stay. The mercury began to quickly rise on my "worry-o-meter."

When I arrived at the center I was tired and hungry after the long cross-country trip but also in awe of the spectacular views and soothing sounds that surrounded me. At meal time, our group was seated around small tables in a dining room that reminded me of home. The exquisite smells that filled the air soon had my mouth watering. The chef came out to tell us about the meal. We learned where the fresh produce had been grown and how it had made its way from the farm to our plates; we took time to appreciate the farmers that had planted the seeds, the rain that had helped the crops flourish, and the people who had helped transport the food from the field to the table. Finally, we learned about the people who had so lovingly prepared the meal that we were about to eat. I was now curious about this meatless feast before me. I visually inspected everything on my plate with the eyes of a child. I took note of the many different smells and savored each bite of this new cuisine. It was one of the most memorable and meaningful meals I've had in my life. Unbeknownst to me, I had just had my first experience with mindful eating.

WHAT ARE YOU HUNGRY FOR?

How often have you taken the time to truly savor a meal like the one described above? Children do this naturally when foods are first introduced. Think back to your experience with your own child when he was younger. He probably picked up the new food, examined it closely, played with it in his hand, and maybe smelled it before placing it in his mouth. Young kids tune in to the sensory experience of eating, and they are more in touch with their hunger, so they know from their internal cues when it's time to start and stop eating. As kids get older and life becomes busier, external cues begin to drive eating behaviors. Your child may eat because it's lunchtime and not because he senses hunger. Over time, kids begin to tune out the internal cues that used to guide their eating.

I find it is common for kids to eat in the absence of hunger, often as a result of distractions during meals. When we sit down as a family to eat meals, we create a social environment to share conversation and good food, and any child is more likely to remember his meal and savor it—eating mindfully— when he eats at the dinner table with his family around and the TV off. Mindful eating is a way to fully experience the act of nourishing your mind, body, and soul. Paying attention to how, what, where, when, and why your child eats will help you to uncover emotional eating (eating to soothe negative emotions) and establish healthier eating habits. See Adam's story for an example of how one child discovered a healthier way to eat through mindfulness.

■ Adam's Story

Adam is a ten-year-old boy who used to spend much of his time with his grandmother after school while his parents worked. His grandmother always made his favorite foods when he was sick. The love she showed him through her cooking made him feel better and meant a lot to Adam.

Then the family had to relocate when Adam's father was reassigned to a job in another city. Adam had to change schools. He had to leave all of his friends, his favorite teacher, and, worst of all, his grandmother. He really missed her. Over the next six months, Adam gained eighteen pounds. His mother tried to limit the snacks that he ate but he started to sneak food into his room and eat alone at night. His mother found candy wrappers and empty potato chip bags under his bed. She knew that Adam was eating even when he wasn't hungry, but she didn't know why.

Adam's parents thought that he might be stressed given all the major changes in his life, so they took him to his pediatrician. During the visit Adam's mother learned that he was indeed stressed, mostly because he missed his grandmother. He cried in the office while talking about how he much missed her, and he said that he ate a lot at night to make himself feel better until he could fall asleep.

Adam's mother helped him learn how to check in with his body to see if he was hungry before he decided to eat the snacks at night. If he was hungry he could have a snack; if not, he would call his grandmother on the phone so he could hear her voice. Adam and his mother also learned how to eat mindfully. This would help Adam slow down while eating his dinner, giving his body a chance to signal that he was no longer hungry. He learned how to identify the internal feelings of satiety and fullness. He would use these internal cues to know when he was full and it was time to stop eating. Adam's mother agreed to get his grandmother's recipes for his favorite foods and make them for him. Adam could then use mindful eating to see how his mother's dishes compared to his grandmother's. Adam liked this idea.

He returned to the office one month later. He had enjoyed the mindful eating practice and had tried two new vegetables using the skills he'd learned. He had found that he liked broccoli and asparagus. More surprising, he had realized he didn't like the potato chips he so often ate at night; the greasy, cardboard taste was less appealing when he ate mindfully. He had also lost two pounds. His mother reported that he seemed more satisfied after dinner and was no longer eating as many snacks before bedtime.

Adam was able to use his mindful eating practice as a way to establish healthier eating habits and explore new foods. Mindful eating is a great way to experience the present moment with your child. Try the exercise below during your child's next meal or snack.

MINDFUL PRACTICE EXERCISE:
Eating a Raisin Mindfully

This exercise is adapted from the original mindful eating exercise in the mindfulness-based stress reduction (MBSR) program developed by Jon Kabat-Zinn and colleagues at the University of Massachusetts Medical School (Kabat-Zinn 1990). A raisin is traditionally used in this MBSR exercise for adults. You may want to experiment with other fruit, such as apple slices.

1. Place two or three raisins (or other available fruit) on a napkin for your child.

2. Tell him to pretend that he's a space explorer visiting from another planet and has never seen a raisin before. Ask him to look at the object on the napkin; what does he notice? If he had to describe this object to someone who had never seen it before, what would he say? You may want to prompt him to notice the color, shape, size, and patterns of the fruit.

3. Next, invite him to pick up the raisin and hold it with his fingers. What does it feel like? What is the temperature, texture, and so on? Ask him to pay attention to what thoughts or feelings he may have about the object. Does he think he will like the way it tastes?

4. Now instruct him to bring the raisin close to his nose and smell it. How does it smell? Tell him to notice if his mouth is watering because he's ready to eat the raisin. Reassure him that there is no right or wrong answer—he's just noticing things about the raisin by paying attention.

5. Get him to put the raisin in his mouth without chewing it. "Notice how it feels in your mouth," you might suggest. Is this what he expected? If not. how is it different?

6. Finally, tell him he may chew the raisin slowly, paying attention to what he tastes as he eats the fruit. He should continue to notice what is happening in his body as he swallows the fruit; what muscles are working? How does he feel as the fruit moves down his throat? Suggest to him, "Think about the raisin traveling all the way down into your stomach, helping to keep you healthy so that you may grow and be strong."

7. Repeat this process of mindful eating with the remainder of the fruit on his napkin.

Next, talk to your child about how he felt during the various stages of this exercise. The following are specific questions to ask:

■ "What did you notice about eating the raisin in this way?"

■ If he's had raisins before, ask, "Did the raisin taste different than it usually does?"

■ "Were you satisfied with eating the raisin in this way?"

■ "What do you imagine it would be like to eat an entire meal this way?"

Remember to use a journal or notebook to record information learned from reflecting on this exercise. Mindful eating helps your child to heighten the senses and appreciate our larger connection with the world through food. Encourage your child to use this practice in his daily life, at school, and at home. When time is limited, he can take a mindful bite using the same process outlined above. Incorporate this practice into your family's routine to model healthy habits for your child.

8

Progressive Muscle Relaxation

Tension is who you think you should
be. Relaxation is who you are.

—Chinese proverb

The body is so wise. There are so many cues that the body offers us, which we can heed if we pay attention. Headaches may be a signal that life has become unbalanced or that we are in a situation that may be detrimental to our health and well-being, for example. Developing a practice that allows you to tune in to these gentle whispers from the body can help you to be more sensitive to subtle internal changes. Your child will be off to a good start if she learns this skill early in life.

LEARNING TO LISTEN TO YOUR BODY

Learning to listen to the body as it speaks to us is a valuable skill. After I began to practice mindfulness I became aware that I hold chronic stress in my neck and shoulder area, resulting in headaches. Taking a pain reliever would temporarily help, but it did not address the underlying problem, my stress. My body was sending a message with these almost daily headaches: my life was out of balance. With continued mindfulness practice I began to notice when my shoulders were tense and elevated before I got the headache. This body signal served as a caution flag for me. When I paid attention and slowed down, I had an opportunity to examine my thoughts and feelings to identify what might be causing my stress. After taking action to address the source of my stress, I found that the headaches gradually decreased in frequency and eventually went away. The same may be true for your child.

YOUR MUSCLES, YOUR FRIENDS

There are more than six hundred muscles in the human body. When you talk about muscles, your child may think of only those she can see, like those in her arms and legs, but of course many of her muscles are deeper inside the body. The smallest muscle is inside the ear and helps us to hear sounds. We use the largest muscle of the body, in our buttocks, every day when walking and sitting. Not all muscles are the same. Some muscles are voluntary; we use these muscles to move our arms, walk, bend, and write. Others are involuntary; these include the muscles in the blood vessels and the heart.

Your child's muscles help her to do many of the activities that she enjoys. When playing video games, using the computer, eating, talking, or dancing, she's using her muscles. Think about how much our muscles support us in all the things that we do every day. It's a good thing for your child to get to know her muscles. Let her know that her muscles are her friends and that she should take care of them so they can continue to support her. Reinforcing the importance of taking care of the body will serve her well for years to come.

■ Susan's Story

Susan was having headaches three to four times per week. It was difficult for her to fall asleep at night. She couldn't relax and fall asleep until she knew her daddy, a police officer, was home from work. Susan watched the news with her mother after dinner. There were almost always two or three reports on shootings each night. "So many people have guns," she would worry. "What if someone tries to shoot my daddy? What if he dies?" These thoughts kept Susan tense during much of the school day. The worries were also there at night when she climbed into bed. Her father had learned about progressive muscle relaxation (PMR) from his doctor. Practicing PMR had really helped his headaches and he wondered if they would help Susan too.

So he asked Susan's doctor to teach her how to use PMR to help her relax. After she practiced PMR every day for two weeks, Susan's headaches went away. It also helped her to get to sleep at night. She still worried about her daddy, but she used PMR and wrote in her journal to ease some of the stress.

PMR can help kids to pay attention to what it feels like when the physical body is relaxed versus when it's tense. Guide your child through the following activity to understand how PMR can promote relaxation and a sense of calm. (Please check with your pediatrician first if your child has any health condition related to the muscles or nervous system.)

MINDFUL PRACTICE EXERCISE:
Getting to Know Your Body

Children are often unaware of how the body responds to the emotional and mental stress we encounter throughout the day. The body scan is used in MBSR to scan for areas of tension and discomfort in the body. It has been found to help relieve stress and chronic pain. In addition, it leads to relaxation throughout the body. This exercise will teach your child how to perform a body scan to look for areas of the body that may hold tension or discomfort. Then, using PMR, she will learn how to release the tension and allow relaxation to enter. (PMR is usually practiced wearing loose clothing and without shoes on.)

1. Have your child lie down on the floor with her legs straight.

2. Say, "We are going to practice tightening and relaxing different muscles in our body. Let's start with the muscles in our right foot."

3. "Notice how your toes feel. Next pay attention to your foot. What are your right foot and toes trying to tell you? Do the muscles feel tight or loose? Is there any pain there? Now, take a deep breath in and squeeze the muscles in your toes and feet, tight, tighter, and tighter for a count of five. Relax and let go of the tension as you release the breath to the count of five. You've just done your first ten pulses. Take a moment to pay attention to how your foot feels. Do you notice any differences now that you've released the tension?"

4. Next, focus on the muscles in the right leg. Ask her to tighten all the muscles in the front and back of her leg, including the calf and thigh muscles, as she takes a deep breath in. Tell her to "make the muscles tight, tighter, and tighter." You can count to five for her or she can count silently to herself. Now she can let go and relax all the muscles that were tight as she exhales to the count of five. Remind her to notice how her right leg feels.

5. Guide her through the remainder of the muscle groups, systematically tensing and relaxing each

muscle group to coordinate with the "in" and "out" breaths. Repeat the sequence above for each muscle group as follows: left foot and leg; belly; right hand and arm; left hand and arm; both shoulders and neck; and face (squeeze the eyelids, tighten the muscles of the forehead, tighten the cheek muscles, bare the teeth, and then relax).

6. For variety, you also have the option of starting with the muscles of the face and working in reverse order to end with the muscles of the right foot and leg.

At the completion of the exercise, ask your child what she learned about her body. What did she enjoy most about this activity? If she found areas of tension or discomfort, explore how she was feeling during the day. Notice any associations between perceived stress or negative emotions (such as anxiety) and the pain or discomfort. This process may help you identify places where your child may "hold stress" in her body. Have her check in periodically throughout the day to see how her body is feeling (relaxed, calm, happy, or sad, for example). Remind her that she can use the tools she's learned today whenever she is feeling worried, stressed, or sad, or when she notices pain or discomfort from holding the worry in her muscles.

It's recommended that adults practice the body scan with PMR while lying down for approximately forty-five minutes. I recommend that kids do the body scan and PMR for ten to fifteen minutes each day as a way to check in with what's going on in the body. This is a great activity to perform as a part of your child's bedtime routine and to help with known stressful situations.

9

Visualization

Seek the key to the problem; the key is within you.

—Philip Arrington

My nephew is an aspiring fashion designer. He can see a gown or swimsuit in his head and create an illustration of it. Once it's on paper he can figure out how to cut and sew fabric to produce a very attractive actual article of clothing. This process of seeing something in the mind and translating those images into reality is a form of visualization. Understanding the power we have to create brings with it a lot of responsibility and a sense of comfort at the same time. If something about life is not working, we can make a different choice. Seeing the new reality in our mind is an essential first step in this process. This chapter will help you teach your child how to harness this creative power.

CREATING A NEW EXPERIENCE

"Today is going to be a bad day." Have you ever started your day with these words? We sometimes spend a considerable amount of time crafting an elaborate story of how things will play out. This happens for kids too. If your child believes he will have a difficult day at school, he may generate thoughts that result in feelings of stress and anxiety, leading to the possibility that his day will be similar to the dreaded day that he had imagined.

Visualization comes naturally to most young children. Using the imagination as a form of play and creativity is the work of children. As kids get older, some of this natural tendency is discouraged ("Stop daydreaming"). While most kids know that they can create a positive world of fantasy, they may not know that they are sometimes creating a negative world full of stress and anxiety. We create our experience through our thoughts, feelings, and actions. Mindfulness can help your child to uncover the thoughts that may be producing much of this stress, in a nonjudgmental way. Visualization can then be used to support the creation of fresh experiences as your child turns insight into new actions.

YOUR DREAMS, YOUR LIFE

Visualization is sometimes described as the language of the unconscious, providing meaningful communication to help you thrive. Athletes use this process to help improve their performance. People in business use it to improve their productivity. Your child can use visualization as well, to help channel his creative energy and help him to achieve positive results in his daily life.

Your child's hopes and dreams help to fuel his motivation to succeed. The practice of visualization can be applied to everyday tasks in your child's life, from playing the piano to standing up to read in front of the class. With practice, he can build confidence in his ability to manage whatever challenges come his way. See how visualization alleviated anxiety and led one child down a path of success.

■ Jay's Story

Jay is a nine-year-old boy who wants to be a race car driver when he grows up. He loves to watch the races on television with his dad; his favorite part is when the winner crosses the finish line and everyone cheers.

Jay came to see me because he was having trouble in school. His mother said he was doing well on his homework assignments, but he was in danger of failing third grade because of his low exam scores. She watched him work really hard to complete his homework and study for tests, but when he sat down to take a test in class it was like his mind would go blank. "I just freeze up," he said.

Before each test, Jay would worry a lot about whether he would do well enough to pass. It sometimes made it difficult for him to sleep well the night before the test. With the end-of-the-year testing coming up, Jay's mother had begun to fear that he might not pass his tests and move on to the next grade. So we decided to help Jay with his test-taking anxiety. I asked Jay to imagine his classroom and picture himself sitting confidently at his desk ready to take the test. After all, he had worked hard to get ready for the test, just like his favorite race car driver would prepare for his race. I told Jay to see himself being calm and relaxed as he took the test, to "feel" the pencil in his hand as he wrote down the answers to the questions with ease. Finally, I invited him to see himself after he'd successfully completed the test, with a crowd of supporters cheering for him, just like the driver at the end of the race. I asked him to take a few moments to just notice how good he felt.

Every night before bed, Jay practiced seeing himself successfully take the exam. Soon, he was sleeping better and he felt much calmer and relaxed in class. His mother called two weeks later to say that Jay had passed his reading test in school. This was the first test he'd passed in a month. He was so proud of himself.

Jay's thoughts that he wasn't smart enough to pass the test had led to feelings of insecurity and resulted in his "freezing up." Visualization allowed Jay to practice paying attention to the connection between these thoughts, his feelings, and his behavior. Visualization was a great tool to help Jay remove some of the worry and self-doubt that were *getting in the way of his success. Practicing helped him to feel prepared to meet the challenges he would face during exam time. It allowed him to gently explore his fears in a safe setting, giving him confidence to keep trying rather than give up.*

MINDFUL PRACTICE EXERCISE: Mind's Eye Adventures

This exercise will teach your child that he can use his thoughts to feel more at ease with negative emotions during times of stress.

1. Have your child sit up tall and straight with his shoulders relaxed. Remind him that he can check in with his body to see how his back and shoulders are feeling as he adjusts his position. If he finds any tension or discomfort, he can use progressive muscle relaxation (PMR) in these areas to help release it.

2. Instruct him to gently close his eyes and notice his breathing. "Imagine a special place where you can go to relax," you say. This may be someplace that your child has visited before, a place he's created in his mind, or a place that is part real and part imagined. Tell him, "It's whatever you want it to be."

3. With his eyes still closed, invite him to look around and explore this place with his mind's eye. You can prompt him with the following questions: "What do you see in this place? What colors do you notice here? Look up and see what is overhead. Look down

and see what is under your feet. Look to your right and left; take in all that you can see. Notice if you are alone or with other people."

4. Now direct him to listen. "What do you hear in this place?" Perhaps he can hear birds or other animals. Maybe he hears voices of other people. Tell him to "tune" his ears to hear the sounds better.

5. "Next you're going to explore this place with your hands," you'll say. "Move around and stretch your hands out in front of you. What things can you touch? Notice how these things feel. Are they smooth or rough? Soft or hard? What is the temperature? Is it hot or cold? Maybe the temperature is exactly right for you, making you feel very comfortable." Give him a few minutes to take in this experience as he checks out the new surroundings in his mind.

6. "Pay special attention to how you feel being in this beautiful place. This is your safe spot. Remember that you can return to this place at any time just by closing your eyes and creating this picture in your mind."

Have your child write in a journal or notebook to reflect on this activity and capture valuable insights he has gained. Specific questions to explore his thoughts and feelings after the exercise include the following: "How did you feel at the beginning of the exercise? What difference do you notice between how you feel now and how you felt at the beginning? What things did you notice most in this safe place? How did you feel while visiting this place? What do you think made this place safe and comfortable?" If your child is younger and not yet writing much, he can use the journal or a plain sheet of paper to draw a picture of his safe space. When he's finished his drawing, give him the opportunity to share his picture with you and tell you about what makes this place special.

Your child can use this practice to take a short mental vacation whenever he needs a break from academic pressures or an overloaded schedule. It's also a great tool to help him access inner wisdom and provide information he needs in order to overcome stumbling blocks and meet desired goals. He can picture his inner adviser, a nurturing guardian who helps him to find the keys to solutions inside of himself. Find other creative ways to build this practice into your child's life.

10

A Mindful Mind

A man is but the product of his thoughts.
What he thinks, he becomes.

—Mahatma Gandhi

Before I learned about mindfulness meditation, I believed that the goal of meditation was to empty the mind. Try as I might, I could not halt the steady stream of thoughts that zipped through my brain. It was a relief to find out that my objective was to notice the thoughts without judgment, rather than to eliminate them.

Thoughts will come and go; that is a part of being human. Making peace with the busyness of the mind can go a long way toward reducing stress for you and your child.

OBSERVING YOUR THOUGHTS

As you are nearing the end of the ten mindful practices, you may be wondering how you are going to implement these strategies into your child's life. Thoughts swirl in your head. "When will I find time to do this? I'm excited about teaching these skills to my child. Maybe I should look for a mindfulness class for myself." The part of you that is aware of these thoughts is being mindful. In fact, one of the most important things I want you to take away from this book is that you are already mindful. And so is your child. However, much of the time we are completely oblivious to the thoughts that are playing in our heads. These thoughts flow through our mind below the radar of our conscious awareness.

At times the opposite is true: there is one thought, or a series of thoughts, that we can't seem to release. We can get caught up in the story of our thoughts as we repeatedly rehash the injustice we believe we've suffered. You may experience this if someone cuts you off in traffic. "I can't believe he cut me off. He must think I'm a real pushover. What if I hadn't hit the brakes in time?" Your child may encounter a similar experience in school when the teacher assigns extra homework to penalize the class for the disruptive behavior of a few students. "Why do I have to do extra homework? I wasn't talking. I didn't get out of my seat. It's not fair that everyone gets into trouble because some kids don't follow the rules." You and your child may each continue to replay the scenario and the accompanying thoughts throughout your day. This persistent worrying and brooding—or "mental rumination"—can be harmful to your child's well-being.

NEW INSIGHTS, NEW INFORMATION

Mindfulness is the observing power of the mind. It is an active process. The increasing awareness that may develop from a consistent mindfulness practice can provide very useful information and messages for your child about her life. She will begin to understand why she feels what she is feeling and why she behaves the way that she does in certain circumstances. This information will also become clearer to you, allowing you to guide and support your child in more positive ways when she is facing a challenge. The openhearted, nonjudgmental nature of mindfulness practice lets a clearer picture of reality come into focus. This acceptance of life as it really is in the present moment often leads to greater feelings of inner peace. With your continued practice, new insights can permit a process of self-discovery as you learn more and more about who you truly are. Developing a deeper mindfulness practice yourself will help you to translate this process for your child and encourage other self-reflective activities to build healthy coping skills.

■ Jennifer's Story

Ten-year-old Jennifer, a very talented artist, loves to paint and sketch pictures on any material she can find. One day, she was cleaning up her acrylic paints when she accidentally spilled one of the containers. Before she could do anything about it, the paint had spattered all over her brother's essay, which was due the next day. Jennifer knew how hard he'd worked on that project. She was very nervous as she walked into his room with the soiled pages in her hand.

"Jason, I accidentally—" she began.

"What did you do?!" Jason shouted. "You ruined my eighth-grade graduation project! Do you know how long it took me to do that? You always mess up everything!"

Jason snatched the paper from Jennifer and slammed his door. Jennifer couldn't seem to get those words out of her head: "You mess up everything." These words played over and over again. Jennifer wasn't aware that this recording was playing in her mind, but her parents and teachers noticed a sharp decline in her confidence. Without her knowing it, these words were affecting how she felt about herself and, ultimately, affecting her performance in school and at home.

When Jennifer came in for an office visit, I asked her what she worried about. "I worry that I'm going to mess things up, and I worry that I'm not going to do a good job." We talked about how those thoughts made her feel: sad and scared.

Jennifer enjoyed blowing bubbles. It was very relaxing to her. We decided to use this image to help her observe her thoughts in a nonjudgmental way. Jennifer learned how to watch her thoughts from a distance. She would place each thought that surfaced in her awareness into a bubble. As she blew on an imagined bubble wand, the thought would be captured in the bubble. She could then watch the bubble drift away until it burst and disappeared. Jennifer used her love of art to record her insights from this practice in a picture journal. It was a great way to combine her artistic talents with her developing mindfulness practice.

This practice reinforced several valuable ideas for Jennifer. First, we are not our thoughts. Second, our thoughts are temporary. The bubbles allowed her to see her thoughts as separate from herself. Watching the bubble burst symbolized the temporary nature of the thoughts and helped her see that it was okay to release them.

Try the mindfulness exercise below to practice observing thoughts with your child.

MINDFUL PRACTICE EXERCISE: Watching Your Thought Clouds

This exercise will help your child learn how to pay attention to the thoughts she's having. One aim of the practice is to encourage kids to slow down and observe the thoughts inside the mind without judgment. Increasing her awareness of what she is thinking creates some space for her to choose how she will respond to her thoughts (if a response is necessary) instead of simply reacting.

1. Have your child sit in a comfortable position. Instruct her to close her eyes and notice her breathing as she begins to relax.

2. Tell her to picture a cloud in her mind. She can nod her head when she has the picture in her mind. Say

to her, "Imagine clouds passing by in front of you, slowly drifting by as they would in the sky." Tell her that each cloud contains information in the form of a thought. Some clouds may contain an emotion along with the thought.

3. "Your job is to watch the clouds pass by and pay attention to what you find inside," you will say. Ask her to notice the thoughts and any emotions she sees inside the clouds as they pass by and drift away. Remind her that whatever thoughts or feelings she notices are okay. She doesn't need to change anything—she's just watching. She should be kind to herself as she notices how she feels about the thoughts and emotions she's observing. Remind her not to judge what she sees. As she notices the information, she may even be impressed or surprised by what she sees.

4. With her eyes closed, she should notice what's in the next cloud. Continue to guide her through this process as she watches each cloud pass by.

5. Your child may become upset if she does not "see" any information contained in her clouds. This sometimes happens. Reassure her that this is okay too. You can tell her that the "empty clouds" may be like silent pauses in conversation; when you're talking to a friend, there are sometimes spaces where no one is talking. These spaces aren't good or bad, they just are what they are. Invite her to welcome the silence and know that the information will appear when she is ready for it.

6. If she becomes distracted during the exercise and is unable to see any clouds, have her return her attention to her breathing for a few breaths and again imagine the next cloud in her mind.

7. Ask her to take three deep breaths and, when she is ready, open her eyes. Parents should close the exercise when the child opens her eyes.

Have your child reflect on this activity in her journal, in a notebook, or simply on a blank sheet of paper. Ask her to draw clouds that contain some of the thoughts and/or feelings that she noticed during the exercise. She may write words or letters in the clouds or she may draw symbols to represent the thoughts or feelings (for example, a smiley face). There is no right or wrong way to do this, so encourage her to do it in the way that is comfortable for her. Once she is finished, ask her to share what she has drawn. You may also want to ask her how she feels about the information that her clouds contained.

Many people have very active minds. Our thoughts can trigger a variety of emotions. If your child thinks that someone believes she is unable to accomplish something, her behavior may reflect that belief. The emotions underlying her thoughts about her own self-worth may go unnoticed, never rising to the surface to be challenged by the truth. This mindful practice of noticing thoughts helps children to realize that the thoughts in the mind may lead to the emotions they are experiencing, ultimately influencing their behaviors.

Teaching your child this skill will provide her with a useful strategy to monitor her mind's activity. With increasing practice she can become more accepting of her thoughts and maintain a greater sense of calm regardless of her external circumstances. For variety, have your child imagine the thoughts being transported by cars driving on a road or imagine them contained in balloons that drift up into the sky. Let your child use her imagination and see what she comes up with.

11

Loving-Kindness

The time will come
When, with elation
you will greet yourself arriving
         at your own door...

—Derek Walcott

What does it mean when we keep our plate so full that we never have time to ourselves? Apart from the time we spend with friends and family, when do we schedule time to be alone? Many people fear being alone and unknowingly create a busy schedule for themselves by overcommitting to work, community, and/or family obligations. Are we afraid to be in our own company? I would challenge you to carve out time to spend with yourself. Notice whether this brings up any feelings of discomfort. If so, there is work to be done. This chapter is a good first step in teaching you and your child to love and appreciate who you truly are.

LEARNING TO LOVE YOURSELF

"I love you." Three very simple words that when put together can mean the world to the person who is on the receiving end of them. How often have you uttered those same three words to yourself and truly meant it? People find it difficult to direct this strong positive emotion inward, focusing instead on the many things that seem wrong with them. Sometimes this is because they regard self-love as selfishness or narcissism. But narcissism is a very superficial love, usually focused on one's physical appearance or mental attributes. The self-love that I am referring to is a healthy appreciation of who we are at our core: the gift that is life itself.

Loving-kindness practice begins with developing a loving acceptance of yourself. In order to truly love someone else, you must first learn to love yourself—not an easy feat for an adult, and even more difficult for a child. Consider a new approach for helping your child get to know and love himself just as he is. Through a loving-kindness practice, he can begin to see past the imperfections and learn to genuinely love and appreciate all the things that make him unique.

SEEING THE LIGHT IN OTHERS

When we begin to see ourselves as we really are, our heart opens and we can see others more authentically. Loving-kindness practice helps us to clean the lens we use to view the world. It allows us to cultivate compassion for others, reflecting back to us what we can now see in ourselves. Take a look at the story below for an example of how nurturing self-love can lead to love spreading through the community.

■ *Bobby's Story*

Bobby, age eleven, came in for a sports physical exam because he wanted to join the basketball team. He liked playing basketball with his older brothers. Bobby was the shortest boy in his class. At his exam, I explained that, since both his mom and his dad were less than average height, he couldn't expect to be as tall as he had hoped. This was bad news for Bobby. The kids at school already teased him and called him "shrimp," and this news was making him think twice about trying out for the basketball team.

I asked Bobby to think about other kids he knew at school and in his neighborhood who were different. We all have something that sets us apart from one another; sometimes it's something you can see (like being tall or short), but at other times it's something on the inside (such as a health condition like asthma or diabetes).

I introduced Bobby to the concepts of loving-kindness and affirmations. Used together, they make a powerful tool for cultivating self-acceptance and unconditional love. Bobby created three affirmations for himself: "I am helpful," "I am unique," and "I am beautiful." I added one that Bobby could work on when he was ready: "I love myself totally and completely." (This last affirmation can be used to start a loving-kindness practice; see the exercise below.)

Bobby knew he'd never become the six-foot-seven pro basketball star he had dreamed of being, but he did leave the office knowing that he could do his best when playing the game and be proud of that. Loving-kindness practice helped Bobby to be more accepting of who he is and to love himself in the process. It also helped him to see other kids' differences in a more positive way and think about how they might feel if he were the one doing the teasing.

Introduce the exercise below to your child. You can both create your own list of affirmations to use before starting the loving-kindness practice.

MINDFUL PRACTICE EXERCISE:
Planting Love Seeds

This exercise is divided into two parts. The first part will show you how to guide your child through a loving-kindness meditation for himself. The second part will help him to send loving-kindness to a loved one of his choosing. I suggest that he start with his closest family members, such as parents, siblings, grandparents, and so on. I would also encourage you to practice both exercises yourself. In your efforts to support your child, it will be important for you to be able to extend genuine loving-kindness to yourself so you know what this feels like. Remember that you will serve as both a positive role model and a guide as he works to cultivate these feelings for himself.

Part 1. Cultivating Loving-Kindness for Self

1. Have your child sit in a relaxed position on the floor. Invite him to close his eyes and notice his breathing as he begins to relax.

2. Say, "I want you to imagine a bright and beautiful sun up in the sky. Feel the warmth of the sun's rays shining down gently on you. The temperature feels just right to you, and sitting in the glow of the sun makes you feel happy."

3. Tell him, "Now picture a small seed in the palm of your hand. This seed is very precious; it contains love. I want you to plant this seed in your heart."

4. Tell him that the sun will shine down on his heart and help the seed to grow. "As the seed grows, it will fill your heart with love—love for yourself and love for others."

5. "We can help the seeds to grow by watering them with 'loving-kindness.'"

6. Ask your child to repeat the following phrases:

   "I love myself just as I am."

"May I be filled with love."

"May I be filled with kindness."

"May I be filled with peace."

"May I be filled with calm."

"May I be filled with patience."

"May I be filled with joy."

"May I be filled with innocence."

Part 2. Cultivating Loving-Kindness for Others

1. Say to your child, "We want the love growing in our hearts to send seeds of love to people we care about so they can plant them in their hearts. We can help other people to grow their love seeds by watering them with loving-kindness."

2. Have your child choose someone close to her to send loving-kindness to (for example, "Mommy and Daddy," "Grandma" or the name of another relative).

3. Ask your child to repeat the following phrases:

   "I love _____ just the way they are."

   "May _____ be filled with love."

   "May _____ be filled with kindness."

   "May _____ be filled with peace."

   "May _____ be filled with calm."

   "May _____ be filled with patience."

"May _____ be filled with joy."

"May _____ be filled with innocence."

Your child may choose to send loving-kindness to other special people in his life (nonrelatives) or even to the family pet. Be flexible and respectful of his wishes.

Loving-kindness is a practice that cultivates compassion for self and others. The more your child practices sending loving-kindness to himself, the more he is likely to find other ways to nurture himself. Create a list of affirmations with your child that record his natural gifts and talents. Aim for at least ten gifts to start. You can add to the list as you identify additional personal strengths for your child, pointing out these gifts and talents as they emerge in his life.

12

The Art of Appreciation

Enjoy the little things in life, for one day you may
look back and realize they were the big things.

—Unknown

"See the good in everything and everyone." This is a message I got early in life. I don't specifically remember anyone ever saying this to me directly; there was just a knowing that it was true. As life brought turbulent times, I would forget this simple truth. It seemed easier to look for negativity to explain the pain I was feeling. I now know that making the effort to appreciate positive things in life helps me learn the lessons that come with the challenges of living. It's a choice. I hope you'll choose to practice the art of appreciation and share this philosophy with your child.

COUNT YOUR BLESSINGS TODAY

It's Saturday morning. In my household, I'm usually the first one up, awakened by the sunlight streaming into the bedroom. The house is so quiet and peaceful at that early hour. Even our dog tends to sleep in on the weekend. Often surrounded by a constant whirr of noise, I appreciate the silence even more in these moments. It dawns on me that if it were not for the almost constant noise in my life, I might not appreciate these gifts of silence when they appear.

How often do we go through our day unaware of all the little gifts that life has to offer? These seemingly ordinary moments are in fact our "presents." Our attention is frequently focused on what we've lost in the past or the desires of our heart that have yet to materialize. Children learn this at an early age. But what would happen if you could help your child to identify all the treasures that are right here in the present moment? Much of the stress that our kids are under results from feelings of lack and inadequacy. Shifting the focus to gratitude and appreciation brings us back to the present moment and reduces stress in the process.

FOCUS ON THE POSITIVE

When I chat with kids in my office, I often hear about all that is going wrong in their lives. This focus on the negative aspects of who we are and the life we lead overshadows all that we have to be grateful for. At first, you and your child may find it hard to identify the things you appreciate. Start with the simple things in life: your breath, your five senses, food to eat, and safe shelter. Once they are introduced to this concept, children quickly learn to find things to appreciate within any environment. When we start to believe that things will go the way we want them to, amazing things can happen. Teaching your child to focus on all that is right in her world gives her a good head start on managing the inevitable challenges that will come her way.

■ Maria's Story

Maria is a six-year-old girl described by her mother as "a worrier." During her last office visit, Maria and I had worked on relaxation breathing. I was eager to learn whether these practices had helped her to be less anxious over the past three months.

When I entered the room, she was smiling and dressed in a beautiful soft pink jumper with matching ribbons in her hair. So I was surprised to learn that the family had become homeless two months earlier, after Maria's father had lost his job. Her mother told me they did not have any extended

*family nearby, so Maria and her mother were living in a
local shelter. Her father had been unable to find another job
locally and was currently working in another state. I guessed
that Maria's anxiety would have escalated during this time,
but, when I asked how she was doing, she told me she was
great because now she got to sleep with her mommy every
night and there were other kids for her to play with at the
shelter. She also proudly told me that she was helping to
teach her mommy the relaxation exercises so she wouldn't
worry so much.*

*I asked her if she could make a list of all the things she
was grateful for. She worked on the list while I talked with
her mother. Before she left the office she had written down
over fifteen items. She said she would have written more
things, but she ran out of room.*

Here was a child who could be lamenting over all that she
had lost, but instead she was able to see the glass as half full.
Maria reminded me that appreciation can help me to look for
the growth opportunity in life's challenges and be grateful for
all that I have in the present moment. In the exercise below,
you and your child will have the opportunity to create a list of
all that you have to be grateful for.

MINDFUL PRACTICE EXERCISE:
Finding Ten Thank-Yous Today

1. Invite your child to play a game with you. Tell her
    that you will search for little gifts that you are given
    throughout the day. The gifts are any people or
    things that she feels grateful to have in her life in

that moment. Provide examples for her from your own life. Perhaps you are grateful that the sun is shining this morning, or you appreciate the kiss that she gave you at breakfast.

2. It may be helpful to track this information as you go throughout the day. A journal or small notebook can work well as a place to jot down your gifts. Younger children can draw pictures or symbols to represent the list of things appreciated; older children can make a simple list, providing details if desired.

3. Set aside some time to share what you've noticed during the day. You can discuss this over the family meal or before bedtime.

In the beginning this activity may seem hard for your child, and possibly for you too. After all, many of us spend so much time focusing on what we're dissatisfied with. Encourage her to be gentle with herself. Ask her to practice mindful breathing and then see what comes to mind. Set a goal to find one thing that you appreciate today.

Start with small blocks of time and build up to an entire day. For instance, say, "I will write down all the things I can think of that I'm grateful for in the next five minutes." As you have your child practice this exercise more often, you may find that it becomes easier for both of you to identify all that you truly have to be grateful for.

You may build upon this exercise by asking your child to notice how she feels when she is focused on what she appreciates in life, as well as how she feels when she is paying attention to what she doesn't have. It's important for children to begin to notice these subtle shifts in emotions based on the thoughts that are being cultivated. Remind her that she can use this exercise as a tool to help her elevate her mood when she's feeling worried, stressed, sad, and so on.

The practice of appreciation is one simple way to help children discover the joy of living in the present moment. Encourage practice of this exercise at least once daily.

PART III

13

Integrating the Ten Mindful Practices into Daily Life

What strengthens mindfulness the most is
the practice of mindfulness itself.

—Jon Kabat-Zinn

After being introduced to mindfulness meditation in 2005, I read voraciously on the subject. There was something about the concept that resonated deep within me. I began educating medical learners about the benefits of mindfulness meditation on health and well-being. I knew a lot of facts and could answer questions about the program, but something was missing.

I hadn't yet fully committed to incorporating the principles of mindfulness into my life. I needed to develop my own personal practice. Once I had done so, I began to notice a difference. With daily practice, the principles were in the forefront of my mind and it became easier to rely on mindfulness when faced with life stress. It was no longer an intellectual exercise but rather a way of being. This may seem like a simple distinction, but I can tell you from experience that it makes a world of difference.

I gained new insights that helped me to better understand why I felt and behaved in certain ways. With this increased awareness, I began to make different choices. I noticed the positive impact in my mood and my sense that all was well, even in the midst of chaotic life circumstances. There was an internal peace that came with regular practice. Others began to see this change as well. Even my son could tell when I wasn't prioritizing my practice. He'd say to me, "Mom, you need to go and meditate." So, not only was this practice helping me, but I was modeling healthy self-care for my son. Introducing mindfulness to children is essential. Providing your child with the support and guidance that he needs in order to build a personal practice is one of the best gifts you can give.

THE IMPORTANCE OF PRACTICE

When you talk to some of the world's best athletes and musicians and ask them about the secret to their success, the common answer is their commitment to practice their craft. Likewise, it's important for your child to practice mindfulness on a regular basis. Mindfulness practice over time allows you to achieve a depth of awareness that is difficult to get when you just rely on theory. Daily practice is one of the best ways to understand the simple fundamentals and value of mindfulness. Even long-time practitioners of mindfulness talk about the importance of practice.

Finding opportunities to use the mindfulness skills you both have learned will help your child to build a meaningful practice. Consistency in practice will help him to reduce nervousness and help keep the skills alive so he's ready to use them when he really needs them. After all, good luck occurs when opportunity meets preparedness. Encourage your child to develop a regular practice using any of the mindful practices in this book. It will certainly help him feel more prepared to handle the inevitable challenges that will come his way.

BUILDING HEALTHY HABITS

After learning new practices, many people are very excited at first. However, life has a funny way of getting in the way of the best intentions. In order to appreciate the power of mindfulness, one must build a daily practice, as discussed above. Any of the ten mindful practices can be used to help develop this practice. It generally takes anywhere from three to six weeks to establish a new habit. Connect the practices with routines that are already established in your schedule, like before a meal or before bedtime. Use the practices to help your child transition from school to home or from one activity to the next. Remember to be gentle with yourself and your child during this time.

I would also recommend establishing a sitting meditation practice, for at least two reasons. The first is that it demonstrates your commitment to yourself: you are a priority. The second is the amazing potential for growth that this practice offers. The sitting provides a break in the constant busyness of our day. Help your child to set aside time to sit during the day, either sitting in silence or sitting to notice his breathing. It is important to provide the support that your child needs to establish a practice; however, do not force your child to sit. All of the practices described in this book are meant to be fun and interactive activities to expose your child to the benefits of mindfulness practice. You may explore his reasons for not wanting to participate and continue to invite him to practice, but the key is for you to be a role model for him by developing and committing to your own personal practice.

REINFORCING NEW CONCEPTS

Remember to use your journal or notebook to capture insights, but also record what worked well in your day that allowed you to practice and what may have gotten in the way. This will provide you with key information to help you find strategies to overcome the obstacles to practice.

Incorporate gentle reminders in and around your child's environment to help establish new routines while building a daily practice. If your child is very visual, perhaps writing affirmations on sticky notes and displaying them prominently in his room or on the bathroom mirror will help to serve as a good reminder. Let him choose the places to display them. If your child is more auditory, setting an alarm or a special ring tone on a cell phone can help to jog his memory. Ask your child what he may need from you to remember to practice. Planning to do the activities together as a family is one way to reinforce these concepts and spend time with your child in the process.

Mindfulness is one path that leads to the same destination: good mental health and well-being for your child. When you are present in your child's life, you are teaching him how to be present too. Mindful parenting is your gift to your child; your child is your present. Commit to the work, have faith in the process, and enjoy the journey!

Resources

MINDFULNESS FOR KIDS

Kaiser-Greenland, S. 2010. *The Mindful Child*. New York: Free Press.

McCurry, C. 2009. *Parenting Your Anxious Child with Mindfulness and Acceptance*. Oakland, CA: New Harbinger Publications.

Saltzman, A. 2007. *Still Quiet Place: Mindfulness for Young Children*. Compact disc. Available at www.stillquietplace.com.

Saltzman, A. 2010. *Still Quiet Place: Mindfulness for Teens*. Compact disc. Available at www.stillquietplace.com.

Shapiro, L. E., and R. K. Sprague. 2009. *The Relaxation & Stress Reduction Workbook for Kids: Help for Children to Cope with Stress, Anxiety & Transitions*. Oakland, CA: New Harbinger Publications.

Smart Dreamzzz CD series: Animal Dreamzzz, Rocky Mountain Day dreamzzz and Dino Dreamzzz, available at www.smart dreamzzz.com, for help with sleep problems.

Thich Nhat Hanh. 2001. *A Pebble for Your Pocket*. Berkeley, CA: Plum Blossom Books.

MBSR PROGRAMS, BOOKS, AND RESOURCES

Center for Mindfulness, University of Massachussetts Medical School. The school's website (www.umassmed.edu/cfm/mbsr) lists more than five hundred practitioners of MBSR.

Kabat-Zinn, J. 1990. *Full Catastrophe Living: Using the Wisdom of Your Body and Mind to Face Stress, Pain, and Illness*. New York: Delacorte Press.

Kabat-Zinn, J. 1994. *Wherever You Go, There You Are: Mindfulness Meditation in Everyday Life*. New York: Hyperion.

MINDFUL EATING

Zeckhausen, D. 2007 *Full Mouse, Empty Mouse: A Tale of Food and Feelings*. Washington DC: Magination Press.

YOGA FOR KIDS

Wenig, M. 2003. *Yogakids: Educating the Whole Child Through Yoga*. New York: Harry Abrams.

Sumar, S. 1998. *Yoga for the Special Child: A Therapeutic Approach for Infants and Children with Down Syndrome, Cerebral Palsy, and Learning Disabilities*. Special Yoga Publications: Evanston, IL.

Wenig, M. YogaKids Fun Collection. Available at www.gaiam.com. YogaKids, yogakids.com.

PROGRAMS FOR HEALTH CARE PROFESSIONALS

Dr. Rachel Naomi Remen (rachelremen.com) is the founder of the Institute for the Study of Health & Illness (ISHI) at Commonweal. This organization provides education and support programs for health professionals who "practice a medicine of service, human connection, and compassionate healing," ishiprograms.org.

Duke Integrative Medicine, Durham, North Carolina, www.duke integrativemedicine.org.

References

American Psychological Association. 2007. Stress in America survey. http://www.apa.org/pubs/info/reports/2007-stress.doc (accessed Jan. 14, 2011).

Benson, Herbert, and Miriam Z. Klipper. 1975/2000. *The Relaxation Response*. Repr. New York: HarperCollins.

Benson-Henry Institute for Mind-Body Medicine. The Relaxation Response. http://www.massgeneral.org/bhi/basics/rr.aspx (accessed October 27, 2010).

Black, D. S., J. Milam, and S. Sussman. 2009. Sitting-meditation interventions among youth: A review of treatment efficacy. *Pediatrics* 124: e532–e541.

Cohen, S., D. Janicki-Deverts, and G. E. Miller. 2007. Psychological stress and disease. *Journal of the American Medical Association* 298: 1685–87.

Cohen, S., and K. A. Matthews. 1987. Social support, Type A behavior and coronary artery disease. *Psychosomatic Medicine* 49: 325–30.

Flook, L., S. L. Smalley, M. J. Kitil, B. M. Galla, S. Kaiser-Greenland, J. Locke, E. Ishijima, and C. Kasari. 2010. Effects of Mindful Awareness Practices on Executive Functions in Elementary School Children. *Journal of Applied School Psychology* 26 (1): 70–95.

Garrison Institute. 2005. *Contemplation and Education: A Survey of Programs Using Contemplative Techniques in K-12 Educational Settings—A Mapping Report.* Garrison, NY: Garrison Institute.

Kabat-Zinn, J. 1990. *Full Catastrophe Living: Using the Wisdom of Your Body and Mind to Face Stress, Pain, and Illness.* New York: Delacorte Press.

McEwen, B. S., and P. J. Gianaros. Central role of the brain in stress and adaptation: Links to socioeconomic status, health, and disease. *Annals of the New York Academy of Sciences* 1186: 190–222.

McEwen, B. S., and E. Stellar. Stress and the Individual. *Arch Intern Med.* 1993; 153(18):2093–2101.

Miller, G. E., S. Cohen, S. Pressman, A. Barkin, B. S. Rabin, and J. Treanor. 2004. Psychological stress and antibody response to influenza vaccination: When is the critical period for stress, and how does it get inside the body? *Psychosomatic Medicine* 66: 207–214.

Ryan, R. M., N. Weinstein, J. Bernstein, K. W. Brown, L. Mistretta, and M. Gagne. 2010. Vitalizing effects of being outdoors and in nature. *Journal of Environmental Psychology* 30 (2): 159 DOI: 10.1016/j.jenvp.2009.10.009.

Wall, R. B. 2005. Tai chi and MBSR in a Boston public middle school. *Journal of Pediatric Health Care* 19 (4) (July–August): 230–37.

Weil, Andrew. 2000. *Eating Well for Optimum Health.* New York: Alfred A. Knopf.

Michelle L. Bailey, MD, FAAP, is a pediatrician who teaches mindfulness-based stress reduction skills to children in Duke Children's Healthy Lifestyles program. She was trained in Dr. Andrew Weil's Fellowship Program in Integrative Medicine at the University of Arizona. She directs educational programs for medical professionals, residents, and students at Duke Integrative Medicine in Durham, NC. Visit her online at www .parentingyourstressedchild.com.